MOITESSIER

A SAILING LEGEND

Books by Bernard Moitessier from Sheridan House

SAILING TO THE REEFS

"Eighty days into a trip, Moitessier and his junk, MARIE-THÉRÈSE, find themselves stuck on the reef at Diego Garcia. Six years later, he and his new love, MARIE-THÉRÈSE II, managed to do it again, this time on the rocks near St. Vincent in the Caribbean. In between these two heartbreaking disasters is a tale of courage, resourcefulness, creativity." *Sailing*

CAPE HORN: THE LOGICAL ROUTE

"This is the story of Bernard and Françoise Moitessier's honeymoon voyage aboard JOSHUA, sailing from Europe to the islands of the Pacific and back by way of Cape Horn, the logical route, which is the fastest way. A true classic by and about one of cruising's best known authors." *Latitudes & Attitudes*

THE LONG WAY

"Moitessier was the original mystical mariner and inventor of the charismatic French boat-bum persona. . . . This account of his most legendary exploit, in which he blew off winning the 1969 Golden Globe round-the-world race so he could 'save his soul' in high southern latitudes, is a bible to ocean sailors with a metaphysical bent. His decision to quit the race and keep on sailing marks the point at which ocean racing and ocean cruising went their separate ways." *Cruising World*

TAMATA AND THE ALLIANCE

"The picaresque life of a seagoing vagabond, a fascinating tale told with remarkable insouciance by the wanderer himself. . . . Risk-taker, romantic, holistic environmental philosopher, biodynamic horticulturalist, husband and father and national hero, and a fine writer to boot—a character who brought brio and dash to all he undertook." *Kirkus Reviews*

A SEA VAGABOND'S WORLD

"A priceless work as straightforward and unpretentious as the man who composed it. . . . No essential topic is left untreated, and the result is a unique window into the way Moitessier the master solved problems that voyagers in the tropics confront all the time. . . . The read is personable and easy going, the format eclectic enough to make every page jump at you with something new and instructive." *Blue Water Sailing*

"Find your boat, fit her out, set sail and sharpen your machete for those coconuts. Moitessier's spirit will be with you." *Classic Boat*

MOITESSIER

A SAILING LEGEND

Jean-Michel Barrault

Translated by Janine Simon

SHERIDAN HOUSE

This translation is dedicated to my mother.—JRS

This edition first published 2005 by
Sheridan House Inc.
145 Palisade Street,
Dobbs Ferry, NY 10522
www.sheridanhouse.com

First published in France
under the title: Moitessier: le long sillage d'un homme libre
by Editions du Seuil

Library of Congress Cataloging-In-Publication Data

Barrault, Jean Michel.
   [Moitessier. English]
      Moitessier : a sailing legend / Jean-Michel Barrault ; translated by
   Jeannine Simon.
         p. cm.
   Includes bibliographical references.
   ISBN 1-57409-204-9 (pbk.)
      1. Moitessier, Bernard. 2. Sailors—France—Biography. 3. Seafaring life.
I. Title.

GV810.92.M65B37 2005
796.124'092—dc22   2004029664

Edited by Jeremy McGeary
Designed by Keata Brewer

Printed in the United States of America
ISBN 1-57409-204-9

Contents

Introduction

Bernard Moitessier was one of my heroes. Not so much for his epic voyages, but for his epic ambivalence and human frailty.

He is probably best known to sailors, and to the non-sailors who have heard of him, as the man who turned his back on probable glory and riches in the 1968-69 Golden Globe Race. One of nine men who set out to be the first to sail alone and non-stop around the world, in the final months of the race, Moitessier appeared to have every chance of winning. But he never turned left after rounding Cape Horn. About the time he was expected in the English Channel, he appeared off Cape Town, South Africa, ranging alongside a ship and sling-shotting (his only method of communicating with the world ashore) onto its deck a can containing the message that he was continuing on west around the world, *"because I am happy at sea, and perhaps also to save my soul."*

For this, Moitessier is certainly better known than he ever would have been had he gone on simply to win, as everyone expected him to. Outside of Britain, he is far better known than English race winner Robin Knox-Johnston. Many set out to conquer hitherto unreached heights—athletes, mountain climbers, sailors, explorers—but few get to within a hair's breadth of succeeding, after marshalling an unbeatable combination of energy, resources, and singlemindedness, to suddenly stop, and turn away, saying, "I'm not really interested after all." This deliberate, almost perverse confounding of his own and others' expectations is what I see as pure Moitessier. This, for me, pulled him out of the pantheon of unsurpassable superheroes, and made him endearingly human.

Moitessier was not a winner in the normal sense. Arrival, finishing a race, completion, were not his thing. Nothing in his life was truer to him than Robert Louis Stevenson's aphorism that it is better to travel hopefully than to arrive. Moitessier only experienced bliss when he was deep in the middle of something, far from its beginning or its end, wrapped up in the purity of the effort itself, whether that was an unparalleled sea voyage or an attempt to get the mayors of small French towns to plant fruit trees.

He can even be seen as an epic loser, for the way he repeatedly and intentionally failed to capitalize on the successes he seemed able to achieve, without design, simply by being himself. When he was—several times—the most famous sailor in the world, and might have become rich and sailed increasingly expensive and sophisticated yachts and aboard them set new sailing records, he turned his back on what he called the "false gods" of fame and fortune and disappeared for decades into Polynesian backwaters, to ruminate, to plant coconut trees, to smoke dope.

Yet he was not unsusceptible to the false gods. He was enormously egotistical, pleased by his fame, the money he earned, the reception of the books he wrote, and the power these gave to his voice. He was also acutely aware and afraid of his susceptibility, and time and again turned away from the wealth (he tried to give away the royalties for one book to the Pope, who refused them), or reputation he had created for himself. This yin and yang aspect of Moitessier's character which forever tore at him and spun him circles, was the result of his formative experiences in two diametrically opposed cultures. Brought up in French Indochina, before this became known as Vietnam, he was exposed as a child to the simple values of his Asian playmates and their families, while at the same time living the privileged life of a European expatriate's son.

His straddle of these two different worlds led him to try to fix the larger, infinitely messier world he discovered as an adult. His attempts to make it a better place, to break through the indifference of societies, and everybody else's perception of the difficulties of doing some good somewhere, were childlike in their hope and naïveté. But he never caught an adult's terminal bug of apathy.

He was certainly bipolar. Unstoppably enthusiastic and grimly depressive by turns, this wire, alternately taut and loose, threaded itself through everything he did and compounded the contradictions of his life and outlook.

MOITESSIER: A SAILING LEGEND

He was an exceptionally attractive man. Not in a pretty, movie star way, but lean, sinewy, masculine, with the face of a philosopher. He was a philosopher, crudely, autodidactically, even tiresomely, but he was also charming, effusive, a magnetic force of a man, and men and women loved him. He gave his women a rough time by normal standards, but they were not normal women. They understood him and loved him and quickly grasped the impossibility of changing him. They all continued unselfishly to love him and came to say goodbye to him when he was dying.

Jean-Michel Barrault was as close and lasting a friend as Moitessier had. His book has nailed him in all his beautiful quixotic complexity. My favorite image from the book is near the end, when the aging, cancer-ridden Moitessier is taken for a spin aboard a mylar and carbon fiber racing sailboat of the latest generation of singlehanders at the start of the world-girdling Vendée Globe race in Brittany—the highly-evolved descendant of the Golden Globe Race. Moitessier, who navigated with a sextant using the sun, moon, and stars, who sailed with no radio, whose JOSHUA was rigged with discarded telephone poles for masts, came from a sailing world more distant from the modern ocean racer's than his was from Columbus's. The sailors with him on that superyacht that day knew it. For a few hours they sailed in company with a man who, despite his best efforts to rub out his own star, had become a living legend, and was responsible, in no small measure, for their own ambitions and achievements.

Peter Nichols
March 2005

MOITESSIER

A Sailing Legend

1

"I am continuing . . ."

"He's mad!"

On March 18, 1969, the watch officer of the small tanker BRITISH ARGOSY moored in Cape Town Bay was alerted by the sound of metal striking metal. Stepping out on the rail, he saw a sailboat, a common sight in the area. With his binoculars he could read the name in large black lettering on the white coachroof: JOSHUA. On its deck, he saw a long-haired man, who with his bushy gray beard looked like a swami, holding a slingshot, aiming at the ship. He repeated to himself:

"This fellow is nuts!"

A skillfully aimed package wrapped in a film container fell on the tanker's bridge. All of a sudden, the merchant officer understood: the missile contained a message. He took out the piece of paper and read,"I am continuing non-stop toward the Pacific Islands because I am happy at sea, and perhaps also to save my soul."

When this message was relayed to Great Britain and France, it brought an identical reaction from most of those who read it.

"He's lost his mind!"

The name of the bearded man who attacked ships with a slingshot was Bernard Moitessier.

Two years prior, Francis Chichester, the winner of the first Solo TransAtlantic Race, had sailed alone around the world stopping once, in Australia. He became a national hero and was knighted by the queen.

The only maritime "first" left to achieve was a solo non-stop circumnavigation. This final challenge required passing through the Roaring Forties with its storms and enormous waves; rounding the three mythical southern capes, Good Hope, Leeuwin, and the Horn; having a sufficient supply of fresh water and food to last eight to 10 months at sea; and despite sailing through the harshest of conditions, avoiding the need for any repairs. Above all, anyone attempting this feat would have to endure loneliness and risk severe physical and mental exhaustion.

Nevertheless several sailors were prepared to give it a try. One of them was Bernard Moitessier, a Frenchman. With his wife Françoise, he had recently completed the longest non-stop passage ever made on a sailboat: 26,000 miles from Tahiti to Alicante via Cape Horn.

In 1968, a British weekly, the *Sunday Times,* proposed the

ultimate race. The wager: a golden globe for the first to finish the race, a check for £5000 for the fastest. The rules were simple: leave from a port in the British Isles between June 1 and October 31 and return after rounding the three capes non-stop and without having received the slightest help. Taking off for a cruise around the world, even non-stop, but at your own rhythm and taking your time is one thing. A race is a very different proposition. Maintaining high speeds against competitors with more skill or sailing faster boats invites greater risk, making it a much more dangerous undertaking. Should a handful of daring sailors accept the wager proposed by the *Sunday Times*, perhaps none of them would come back alive.

Nevertheless, nine competitors did start: six British, one Italian and two French sailors, Bernard Moitessier and his friend Loïck Fougeron. On June 14, Robin Knox-Johnston, an officer in the British Merchant Navy, was one of the first to set off. The bragging in the French press after Eric Tabarly's victory in the 1964 transatlantic race had so infuriated Knox-Johnston that upon hearing of the race organized by the *Sunday Times*, he proclaimed: "In all fairness, by right a British sailor has to be the winner."

Five of the contestants sustained damage and abandoned the race even before reaching the Cape of Good Hope. On a modest ketch, Knox-Johnston made slow progress. Two other British competitors left very late on trimarans and didn't appear to present much of a threat: one was disappointingly slow and the other's progress seemed erratic—Chichester, the president of the race committee, had trouble believing the positions reported by its skipper.

Moitessier had left on August 22. He had no radio transmitter on board—the race committee and family and friends had to rely on chance encounters to get news. His red ketch was sighted off the Cape of Good Hope, off Tasmania, and finally on February 10, 1969, off the Falkland Islands. He had rounded Cape Horn and was quickly catching up on his main adversary, Robin Knox-Johnston, who had passed the Falklands on January 23. The Frenchman had gained 67 days. All Moitessier had to do was to continue north up the Atlantic, an easy sail in the trade winds for someone who had survived the killing storms of the Southern Ocean.

It appeared certain that Moitessier would reach Plymouth on or about April 15 and be the big winner. He would get the check for 5,000 pounds sterling—which this cash-poor sailor needed badly—and receive the Golden Globe trophy for being the first to sail solo, non-stop, around the world. A triumphal welcome was being prepared—an armada of warships and pleasure boats was standing by to cross the English Channel to escort the returning hero as he completed the final miles. He would most likely receive the Légion d'honneur, France's prestigious decoration.

And now, the sailor who was awaited in Ouessant, off Brittany, had shown up off Cape Town announcing that he was *continuing non-stop toward the Pacific*. Had the months of loneliness combined with the harsh conditions in the southern ocean affected his mind? His wife Françoise, who had been counting the days until he came back, sighed, "This is long, this is very long." Now, responding to a question by the newspaper *L'Aurore*, she admitted: "I don't understand." Francis Chichester was skeptical: "This doesn't make any sense. This is not like Bernard Moitessier. Nevertheless it can't be a joke."

On March 18, at 8:30 a.m., the harbor patrol boat ELIZA-BETH R was at the northeast end of Tall Bay, off Cape Town. Captain Trevor di Angelo spotted the reflection of a signal mirror coming from a red ketch at anchor with its sails furled. He told the story: "A tanned, bearded man, looking physically very fit, hailed us. He said to us, 'I am Moitessier.'" The sailor indicated that he did not want to be boarded. He threw onto the bridge of the patrol boat a waterproof container with a package inside addressed to Jacques Arthaud, a message to the French Consul, and a letter for the President of the Royal Cape Town Yacht Club. Moitessier confirmed: "I am continuing." After waving good-bye to the harbor patrol crew, he set sail, headed toward BRITISH ARGOSY and then veered south.

Had he reached some kind of nirvana on the high seas and lost all common sense? On land, everyone was worried. Françoise, assuming that her husband knew nothing about his competitors, persuaded the South African radio station to send him a message that he was winning. It never reached Bernard. On March 20, L'Aurore, announcing Moitessier's decision based on the still incomplete information the paper had received, printed an article under the title: "To try a second circumnavigation . . ." According to the daily paper, Françoise who had rounded Cape Horn with her husband and faced a terrible storm in the South Pacific with him, expressed her fears: "I know only too well all the hardships of such an endeavor." Some suggested sending a patrol boat from Cape

Town after the sailboat to beg Moitessier to reconsider, to go back and forget this dangerous, nonsensical enterprise.

There was good reason to worry. Fall was approaching in the Southern Hemisphere, and with it the bad weather, the cold, the shorter days, the mist, and the threat of icebergs. Moitessier could run out of food. Would the gear, the rigging, the sails, having endured one circumnavigation, stand up to another? And what about the man himself? The captain of BRITISH ARGOSY said he seemed in good shape. But would he not reach the limits of his endurance, exhausted by so many months on the most dangerous oceans of the world? And where was he taking his ketch? Did he intend to round Cape Horn again? Would he try another non-stop round-the-world voyage?

What was Moitessier looking for? Who was this man who could turn his back on gold and glory to face the extreme loneliness of the Southern Ocean all over again?

2

Childhood in Indochina

Bernard Moitessier's childhood and his adolescence partly explain his refusal to win the round-the-world race and his decision to turn his back on Europe and what he called "its false gods."

His father, Robert Moitessier, belonged to a family of intellectuals and had a business degree from the Hautes Etudes Commerciales. He married Marthe Gerber, who had studied art at the Beaux Arts. The couple left France shortly after their wedding. Robert Moitessier had a good business sense and within a short time built a prosperous import-export business in Indochina. In the 1930s, during the Depression, he bought land cheaply in areas where he felt Saigon would develop, and sold them later at a large profit. Knowing war was coming, he stocked up, filling every space he could find both at home and in the warehouses with merchandise: cartons of Ovaltine, Chauve-Souris wine, condensed milk. Many years later, Ovaltine would still be, along with rice, one of the main ingredients of Bernard's onboard diet.

Bernard was born in Hanoi, April 10, 1925, a few weeks after his parents arrived in Indochina. Two more boys, Françou and Jacky, followed, each at a year's interval, and the three of them became a gang of mischief-makers. Elisabeth, born nine years after Bernard, and Gilbert, born in 1938, were much less involved in the escapades of their older siblings.

In his book *Tamata and the Alliance*, published shortly before his death, Moitessier described in a broad canvas and with great detail the influence the 20 formative years in Indochina had on him. From an early age, he liked to run around the market in Saigon, to mix in with the life of the crowds, smell the aromas, and eat a Chinese soup while squatting on his heels. He enjoyed wandering the river banks looking at the junks. One day, the captain, the *taî cong*, of one of the junks, impressed with the young boy's curiosity and surprised by his knowledge of Vietnamese, invited him on board. The *taî cong*'s tender was a round floating basket made of braided bamboo that he sculled with a paddle, pulling instead of pushing. Many years later, Moitessier remembered this when he used a truck inner tube as a dinghy. Even then, the child was dreaming: *"I would give anything to sail away aboard this junk, far from school . . ."*[1]

Bernard, Françou, and Jacky were free spirits and didn't enjoy school. Their father, exasperated by their report cards, whipped them, because "after three generations of intellectuals," they didn't measure up to his standards. Bernard, aged 11, had to write an essay in history class on Napoleon's Egyptian Campaign. Ignoring Napoleon (and mistaking the word campaign, which in French also means the countryside), he described a country strewn with pyramids and watered by the Nile, thus gaining an entry in Jean-Charles *The Dunces' Book.* Another essay on the topic "A rolling stone gathers no moss" provoked this comment by his teacher, "You are not only a lazy dunce, but a cretin and an incorrigible. Boys like you never amount to anything in life. You are something of an anarchist." Sincere and naïve, the student had developed a theme in which he believed that *"the more you move, the more you travel, the more different things you do in life, the less you risk getting infected with bad habits."*[2]

Bernard's mother, Mamette, was well read, happy and had an artistic nature. The message she imparted to her children was rich in philosophy, kindness and wisdom. *"My mother,"* said Bernard, *"wanted us to grow into handsome little animals full of life and health, with sharp eyes, and quick on our feet."*[3] Their father shared that ideal. Beneath a severe appearance, he had a tender heart. He enjoyed sports, he played rugby and water polo, and set records swimming under water. His sons tried to emulate him, jogging the one and a half miles to school through the streets of Saigon, in those days lined with fruit trees, mango trees, and tamarind. After school and on Sundays, Bernard, Françou, and Jacky spent hours at the swimming pool, and even sneaked in over the fence at night to do laps. At the age of 6 or 7, Bernard could do the crawl non-stop for three miles and would swim until his father forced him out of the pool. He played water polo. But Françou was the best swimmer and became the school champion in the 100 meters.

If the teachers despaired of them, it was because the boys felt that real life lay elsewhere. During class, they drew junks in the margins of their exercise books. *"We were dunces and delinquents, my brothers and I,"* Bernard admitted, *"dreaming of the sea and the forest, and of freedom, while stuck in a kind of torpor broken only by crises in which despair and rebellion went hand in hand."*[4]

Their imaginations took them to the Gulf of Siam. Every summer they spent two months in a fishing village, near Rach Gia, where they would arrive after a marvelous three-day drive through the rice paddies of Cochin China in the large family car, a Hotchkiss. For the boys it was a time of discovery, of adventure shared with their village friends, Xaï, Phuoc, Kieu, and Hao. Squatting on the platforms in the huts, they shared rice soup flavored with spicy *nuoc mam*. Assam, their Chinese *amah*, taught them to beware of the *Ma Qui*, the meanest of all spirits. They explored the forest, set traps, and chased the flying lizards. Bernard's favorite weapon was the slingshot. It was his constant companion, his "religion," as he called it. He was incredibly skilled with it and he practiced all the time, on anything that moved in the village as well as on the Saigon street lamps.

The boys hung out with the fishermen, who taught them how to take care of their canoes. Bernard watched Phuoc's father as, with a hatchet and a red-hot iron, he skillfully crafted an anchor made out of hardwood and held together by angled wooden pins: although the joint might loosen over time, the flukes and shank would stay connected.

Just before the season the fishermen caulked their junks. Bernard followed Hao's father everywhere, like a shadow, *"hypnotized by his magician's hands."*[5] To really caulk properly, the carpenter explained, "you have to enter the crack along with the fiber, become the fiber itself." The adolescent tried to imitate the man's technique, to enter the crack. It was a lesson he never forgot. Alongside the villagers, the three boys prepared the fishing lines and the hooks. Their reward was to go aboard the junks. *"Great outings in the wind of the open sea, camping on desert islands, light breezes and strong winds, reefing in the squalls, boat drunk with wind, sea, and sun."*[6]

Speaking perfect Vietnamese, he understood this centuries-old culture; he discovered that Chinese characters allow two people who don't speak the same language to understand each other by drawing ideograms. One day, he gave Phuoc's father a compass. The fisherman had never seen this magical instrument, with its needle that allowed you to find your way even at night. He was fascinated and turned it in his hand for hours. The next day he returned it to Bernard. He had thought it over: *"You need light to use this thing at night, and that blinds you. But with the stars or the direction of the waves or the wind, you can always tell where you are going, and your ears stay open to hear what the sea is saying."*[7]

Many years later, when Bernard took students sailing, he taught them to use their senses to help them navigate. An old monk, close to death, passed to him a final message of guidance: There are three stages in the school of life, and before entering the school of "transmitting," you have to have first passed through the school of "seeing" and that of "doing."

Sadly, the holidays came to an end. When Bernard was 15, his father, angered with his bad grades in school, registered him at Saigon's vocational high school. He was expelled before the end of the year. Luckily a small agricultural school accepted him and under its more liberal regime the rebel youth found happiness. At 18, he was hired as supervisor in a rubber plantation. He began to pinch his pennies, because his childhood dream to build a boat and travel all over the world was very much alive.

But the time for it had not yet come. When Bernard turned 19, his father hired him to work in the family business, with the expectation that his eldest son would one day succeed him. His future would have been assured, but the young man felt he had *"to choose between staying on my comfortable branch or overcoming my fear and letting go, jumping into the unknown."*[8] He enjoyed the trips to visit customers in the villages, but he couldn't stand the day-to-day routine of processing invoices in an office. To his father's dismay, he chose independence, and returned to the village of his holidays.

All he thought about was the sea and boats and the idea of sailing the oceans to discover faraway islands. He and Xaï found a fishing junk that they bought and outfitted together. In Rach Gia, while completing the provisioning of the junk, he met Abadie, a Frenchman who had fought in Verdun in World War I and had led a life of adventure. Abadie became a sort of spiritual father for the young man. Contrary to Bernard's real father, Abadie believed that life, freedom, and independence could teach far more important lessons than anything learned within the walls of a regular school. Bernard was seduced. Abadie took him on his junk, TITETTE, for a cruise to nearby islands. It was a time of sheer joy.

But they came back to a dramatically changed world.

The happy and carefree days were gone. Paradise suddenly became hell. In 1940, France had lost the war. Now, the Japanese had invaded Indochina. Japanese soldiers, yelling, their guns aimed at Abadie and Moitessier, boarded TITETTE upon their return. Bernard, slow to put his hands up, was almost shot. Both were made prisoners, their hands tied. Later, as soon as he was freed, Bernard joined his mother, his two younger brothers, and his sister in the village. They returned to Saigon. His father, a reserve officer, was in prison. Bernard became the head of the family.

After Hiroshima, everyone wondered if Japan would capitulate. Many believed so, but the Japanese still occupied Indochina. Bernard then engaged in an idiotic act of patriotism: he raised the French flag on the balcony of the family home. The Japanese police came to the house, arrested the family and everyone else there at the time, and threw them in jail.

His mother knelt in a corner of the cell; Abadie, Françou, and Jackie didn't move. A Japanese officer, his hand on his holster, stood in front of Bernard and fixed him with a stare. "Today I am twenty years old," Bernard thought, "and I am going to die." They faced each other, eye to eye, for a long time. The officer spared the young man. They were held for three days in the cell, then in jail for three weeks. When he was released after six months in a Japanese jail, Bernard's father looked at 45 like a wizened old man.

Japan surrendered. But would Indochina return to its happy, peaceful prosperity? Violent movements for independence rose up; the killings escalated. When the Armistice Commission came, the communist Viet Minh organized a massive anti-French demonstration that ended in a bloodbath. Murderous confrontations erupted among the Indochinese who wanted to get rid of the French settlers, those who wanted the French to stay, and the French colonizers who hoped to reinstate their pre-war dominance.

Former playmates and former schoolmates became enemies, resulting in a terrible massacre of innocent people. With his two brothers, Bernard joined the Volunteer Liberation Group and went on patrols led by Abadie. When he was mobilized, he was assigned to the GAZELLE, a 600-ton gunboat, as a seaman and interpreter. On missions in the Mekong and in the riverbanks, Bernard took part in the fighting. *"But when I had the chance to shoot a Viet, I would shift my aim at the last instant so the bullet would brush by him, hammering in his ear, and he would only be frightened."*[9]

Symbolic of the horror of those times, a tragedy took place in the village of his childhood where he'd known only happiness and friendship. Xaï had revealed that Baï Ma was hiding a gun. Françou and Jacky, leading a company of Cambodian snipers, arrived at dawn. In front of the whole village, Françou killed Baï Ma with a shot to the head. The huts were set on fire. The story forever haunted Bernard: *"When Françou told me about it, without apparent regret, hatred still in his eyes, I knew that we had truly lost our country. It was as if he had killed his own brother.*"[10] Françou committed suicide shortly after. Jacky left for Guyana.

For the eldest of the three brothers who had been so close, this bloody rupture from the world of his childhood gave rise to an oppressive "Dragon" of remorse that would accompany him throughout his life and refuse to die.

After a fresh attempt at working for his father, Bernard decided to go back to his beloved Gulf of Siam. He set up a business sailing cargo between Rach Gia and Kampot, Cambodia. He would load a big junk with 20 tons of rice in Cochin China, transport it to Cambodia, and head back with a cargo of wood or palm sugar. He was happy aboard this vessel with its slatted sails, and he called that period the richest and most formative of his life. But six months later, when the French Sûreté suspected him of trafficking arms for the Viets, he had to stop. He persuaded his father to grant him a six-month leave at half pay, and bicycled and hitchhiked through France and Europe. This was a new world for him, but he was dismayed to find fences around gardens and plane trees along the roads instead of the fruit trees of Indochina.

On the ship going back to Saigon, he met a young woman with golden hair. Marie-Thérèse would be his first love; they became engaged, but he broke it off. *"I was afraid to find myself trapped with a wife and children in an Indochina full of violence ... I behaved like a bastard, but Marie-Thérèse would always be in my heart."*[11]

He returned to learn that Xaï had been killed and Abadie

had been murdered by the Viet Minh underground. By some miracle or another, Bernard had escaped, for the third time. Working once more for his father, he spent his free time studying English, Spanish, Russian, and Chinese characters. He was more than ever determined to go to sea. This dream would soon be realized in a boat called SNARK and, later, in a junk that, true to the love of his youth, he would name MARIE-THÉRÈSE.

———— ∞∞∞ ————

1, 2, 3, 4, 5, 6, 7, 8, 9, 10, 11. *Tamata and the Alliance.*

3

---∞∞∞---

"Because I am
happy at sea . . ."

In the message he had sent with his slingshot onto the bridge of BRITISH ARGOSY, Moitessier explained: "I am continuing because I am happy at sea." He had discovered the joy of sailing with the fishermen of the Gulf of Siam. The trip on Abadie's junk was *my first long sailing trip, and I didn't have anything to do except take it easy, seemingly forever.*[1] Night had fallen, Abadie was resting below, and Bernard was steering, skippering the boat. *"It was a magic that renewed within me my alliance with the universe . . . I wanted to be alone and have the whole boat to myself, alone with the sea. . . . I dreamed of sailing away someday in my own boat, very far and perhaps alone."*[2]

What for most amateur sailors is an enjoyable pastime was for Moitessier a passion, a way of life, the means by which to discover the planet, the key to freedom. Sailing an oceangoing boat gave him the means to flee this new country; the Indochina of his childhood and youth was gone. This country had broken his father and killed Abadie, his spiritual guide. Xaï was dead, Baï Ma was dead, Françou, the poet, was full of hatred.

A miracle appeared in Saigon Harbor. A 40-foot ketch, SNARK, was for sale, offering him the world. Sure it needed work, but it was too good an opportunity. Bernard's first associate let him down: he was a day dreamer, not ready to leave.

He soon found a new partner willing to share in the expenses of fitting out. Nothing in their first meeting led him to think that Pierre Deshumeurs would become his mate: *"A dandy who spoke like a book, Deshumeurs was impeccably turned out in rayon pants with knife-edge creases, a monogrammed silk shirt, a large pinky ring and very narrow patent-leather shoes. Nothing about him appealed to me."*[3] Nevertheless, a few months later, they cast off with Deshumeurs on board and they got along right from the start. Bernard expressed his joy at being at anchor in an archipelago off the coast of Malaysia. *"SNARK slept like a bird with its head under its wing, in a blue-green nest surrounded by flower-like coral reefs at the bottom of a tiny bay whose pebble beach was lined with palm trees."*[4] They lingered on.

Only the long sailing passages to get there could compare with the seduction of the tropical islands. *"Today I feel happy, well fed, and full of wonder. I am living intensely . . . How delightful it is to be able to live in peace, to read, write, cook, listen to music, or simply dream under the stars, while you watch the phosphorescent wake grow as it stretches out astern."*[5]

SNARK was rotten, and the two captains did not always get

along. After cruising to Singapore and Malaysia and returning to Indochina, all the while pumping constantly to keep the leaking boat afloat, they sold SNARK. After liquidating some stocks that he still had in his father's business, Bernard bought a junk, named her MARIE-THÉRÈSE, spent the last of his money to fix her up, and left, heading west. Ever since his childhood when he read Gerbault, Robert Louis Stevenson, and Conrad, he'd dreamed of going to the Pacific Islands. He turned his back on Indochina and, perhaps, on the Dragon of his nightmares.

On his thirteenth day at sea he discovered a new happiness. *"I was slowly beginning to realize what a huge treasure solitude had brought me. At last, I had time to be alone with myself, time to contemplate what was around me. Before, everything had been a blur. During all those years I had never stopped running. And now a great calm had been spreading within me, a calm I could savor."*[6] Moitessier was 27. This was the first time he'd set off solo, and he had no other aim than to be at sea with all the world's ports of call before him. Already beginning to form in his mind was the germ of the reasoning that, 17 years later, would bring him to that decision: "I am continuing . . ."

Yet sailing and feeling the master of the world, in total harmony with his boat, could not last forever. The beautiful adventure threatened to end in Singapore, where MARIE-THÉRÈSE put in after crossing the Gulf of Siam. One night, Bernard slept ashore, and on returning to the boat found she had sprung a leak and was sinking. He towed her to shore and beached her. *"There wasn't anything I could do. I was screwed; I didn't have any money, and I didn't know which way to turn."*[7] But Bernard had already proven very lucky, and would continue to be so when he needed help later on. Fate stepped in. A ship chandler put his hand on his shoulder: *"Pump all night. I will be here to morrow morning when the tide starts to ebb."*[8] The man kept his word and arrived at dawn with a crew of caulkers. MARIE-THÉRÈSE was saved. *"He said that what he had done for me was exactly what someone had done for him, at a time when he couldn't see a glimmer of hope. So I didn't owe him anything, but I shouldn't forget to pass this gift on someday."*[9] This was the same message the old dying monk had given him: the "school of transmitting."

Losing his boat would have been a tragedy. In *Sailing to the Reefs*, his first book, Bernard wrote, *"I had quite simply fallen in love with this beautiful junk from the Gulf of Siam, with her bold and sturdy lines, fragrant with natural oil."*[10] Besides MARIE-THÉRÈSE had a unique advantage. All solo sailors find it impossible to be constantly at the helm. They need time to sleep, eat, or simply sit back to contemplate the sea, the sky, and the birds. Joshua Slocum, the first man to sail alone around the world, was lucky: His yawl SPRAY kept her course by herself on all points of sail. *"MARIE-THÉRÈSE had been doing this for weeks . . . I am really proud of this boat."*[11]

Bernard had not left Indochina voluntarily, but as Baudelaire wrote, "If you can stay, stay; but if you must, go." His only navigational instruments were a compass and a sextant. He had no log on board to measure distance, no chronometer to calculate longitude, no radio, no motor, and no electricity. Moitessier set sail trusting his seaman's instinct to interpret signs in the sky, in the sea, and from the birds, just as in the days of Columbus.

In earlier days the Arab dhows trading between Asia and the Middle East took advantage of the alternating monsoons to benefit from favorable winds. Moitessier would have a rough passage, but he had only himself to blame. He stayed too long in Singapore and missed his chance. Leaving the Strait of Malacca, he was sailing against the southwest monsoon and met a wall of wind and confused seas. Sailing into the wind was not MARIE-THÉRÈSE's greatest strength. The struggle lasted six weeks. Bernard encountered "an eternity of headwinds and squalls" and he saw himself turning into a sort of aquatic animal with its sole imperative to hang on, come what may.

Finally MARIE-THÉRÈSE reached the trade winds, and sailed on, in gentle following winds with the helm lashed. This was paradise. But Moitessier had made another mistake. He had originally planned to go to Madagascar, but a man he called Uncle James, who had helped him out, had asked him as a favor to bring to the Seychelles an ebony table that was too heavy to be taken on the plane.

When sailing, it's always dangerous to subject yourself to constraints on your schedule or your route. A passage to Madagascar would have been free of hazards and making landfall on that large island with its high mountains would have been easy. The Seychelles route was much more difficult. A dangerous coral archipelago, Chagos, lay across the route. It had no lighthouse, and by day the only part visible from a distance of 10 miles was Diego Garcia, a large atoll at the southern tip.

Having neither a watch nor a log, Moitessier could determine only his latitude. Even if he'd had a chronometer or a

fairly accurate watch, he didn't know enough celestial navigation to calculate his position exactly. He could only hope that
his course would keep him a safe distance from dangers, and
that the flight paths of birds would warn him of the proximity
of islands. He trusted his instinct, but received no forewarning.
Sixty-five days after leaving Singapore, at night, MARIE-THÉRÈSE
crashed onto the reef. By dawn, the boat was destroyed, her
hull stove in. *"Leaning my cheek against her lovely bows, lifeless
now, I wept. I wept for my memories, my books, for the loss of this
boundless world, made up of dreams and action."*[12]

Three years later, Bernard was at the helm of a new boat,
MARIE-THÉRÈSE II. The ketch was in dry dock in Martinique
when Moitessier received a telegram, "Arrive Trinidad in four
days." The message was from Joyce, a young woman whom
Moitessier had become close to in Cape Town and who was
now ready to share the life of a sea vagabond. On leaving Saint
Helena he'd felt sad. *"For the first time, I was feeling lonely at
sea."*[13] He wrote Joyce, asking her to meet him in the West Indies. Joyce had a difficult time finding a cargo ship to take her
there: The few ships that made that passage had little available
space for passengers. The telegram left him only a few days to
reach Trinidad, and MARIE-THÉRÈSE II was still high and dry.

As soon as MARIE-THÉRÈSE II was back in the water,
Bernard set sail. This was foolish. The Caribbean has very few
lighthouses, night sailing was dangerous, and Bernard was exhausted. He had hardly slept the night before because of the
mosquitoes that had invaded the cabin while he was in the
shipyard. He stood watch in the channel between Martinique

and St. Lucia, and when he set a course for the west coast of St. Vincent, he was on his third night without sleep.

In the pitch-black night, Moitessier couldn't see anything. There was no lighthouse on the northern end of St. Vincent. He decided to sleep for an hour and a half. *"It was almost two o'clock. A violent crash woke me . . . A second crash shook the boat. And then suddenly another one, accompanied by a dreadful cracking of tortured wood."*[14]

As once before, after the loss of his first sailboat, he who had believed himself to have a god-given ability as a sailor, had been rudely brought back to reality. *"There was no Old Salt anymore. There had never been an Old Salt. Just a poor jerk sobbing as he watched his beautiful* MARIE-THÉRÈSE *being torn apart in the middle of the night on the Diego Garcia reef."*[15]

The same drama was unfolding again. *"Every impact as she struck the rock went straight to my heart and tore at my innards. And there I remained, paralyzed, clinging to the mainmast and clasping for the last time what had been my boat, the most beautiful boat in the world."*[16]

———❧———

1, 2, 3, 4, 6, 7, 8, 9, 15. *Tamata and the Alliance.*
5, 10, 11, 12, 13, 14, 16. *Sailing to the Reefs.*

4

Teachers and Guides

That young man who thought he was the master of the universe found himself virtually naked, broke, and without a boat—shipwrecked both mentally and physically. The natural reaction of most people, safe in their carefully ordered lives, should have been to say that he asked for it. He got no more than he deserved. He thinks he's so smart, let him take care of himself.

People responded quite differently to Moitessier's distress. In Diego Garcia, on Mauritius, everywhere he needed help, he found it. In 1952, Bernard was an attractive young man of 27, 5 feet 10 inches tall, thin, and muscular from swimming and physical exercise. Something about him prompted people to lend him a hand, even without his asking. His charisma, his charm, and perhaps even his aura were factors, but there was more to him. Those charmed by Bernard were attracted by what they saw in him: his energy, his willingness to take risks, his tenacity, his optimism, his independence, and his desire to achieve harmony with the world around him. He dared to do what others who lacked courage or the opportunity could only dream about. It was perhaps this quality in him that Tha, the boss at the rubber tree plantation where he had worked, had recognized. Bernard, 19 years when he left, had said good-bye and thanked him, drawing the traditional Buddhist response: *"I told him that I would never forget the earth, even if I went far away someday . . . When we parted, he knelt down, touching his forehead to the ground. That meant, 'I greet the god within you.'"*[1]

The fishermen on Diego Garcia were not that introspective. Very simply they were generous, as poor people can be. They took him in like a family member. Not only had he saved his neck, thanks to their friendship, he found *"joy, release from anxiety, and peace."*[2]

Two months after losing his boat, Moitessier landed in Mauritius, hoping to work his way home on a cargo ship. The French consul, "a cool guy," urged him to stay on the island for a while. Several people helped him to get a job and finance the publication of his ship's log. He gave lectures. Very quickly, he made friends.

A prominent local family offered him lodging, treating him like a family member. Emile Labat, a descendant of one of the old French aristocratic families that had settled the island, invited him to stay at *Port d'Attache* ("home port"), his residence at the seashore. The castaway had found a second family. He started work overseeing charcoal burning in a sugar plantation, but got soon bored.

He noticed that the reefs were teeming with fish, but they refused to be caught on a fishing line. He was a strong swimmer, and found he could hunt them easily while diving. He made enormous catches of 80 to 100 pounds daily, which he sold at the market in Saint Louis. In a month, he was almost rich. Then one day he felt a terrible pain in his right foot, "as though it was being crushed in a vice." A shark had taken hold of it. *"By a reflex action I struck him a violent blow on the head with the butt."*[3] It was time for another miracle. Moitessier was hospitalized and operated on. His foot was saved. A month later, he was able to walk and even to run.

In *Sailing to the Reefs*, Moitessier wrote at length about the incident, describing the behavior of sharks and providing useful tips for divers. But for the time being, that was the end of his spear fishing. Bernard was hired to manage a fishing and guano business in the Cargados-Carajos Archipelago, a group of coral islands 240 miles from Mauritius. When he returned 10 months later, he had saved quite a bit of money.

He had to decide whether or not to stay on this island which promised a peaceful life among its generous and friendly people. Coming after the hardships on board MARIE-THÉRÈSE and her tragic end, this would have been a wise move. But the old dream was still alive. Just as he'd turned down a career in his father's business, and broken off his engagement with the girl he loved because he was afraid of marriage and commitment, he decided to resist the charm of this tropical island and abandon his new friends. Despite the setbacks, Bernard was following his dreams.

Drawn to the sea and long voyages as strongly as ever, Moitessier undertook the building of a sailboat to replace MARIE-THÉRÈSE. Timber was hard to come by on Mauritius but friends were able to find what he needed, some of it in invaluable curved lengths, at a cost of next to nothing.

With the help of a local carpenter, the project proceeded, part inspiration, part improvisation "eastern style." Nothing was drawn on paper, it was all done by eye. First the long keel was laid on its parallel supports, then the stem and sternpost were fitted at appropriate angles and at a distance apart that would determine the length of the boat. They cut the midships frame and the carpenter offered it up. Bernard, judging it by eye, would tell him, "Open it up a little. No, not so much." When the angle looked right, they fastened the frame in place. After two more frames were set up, they had a good idea of the shape the boat was taking. Thin flexible battens gave a more general idea of the shape and how the planking would lie.

In nine months, MARIE-THÉRÈSE II was built. She was a 28-foot ketch with a 10-foot beam and a Norwegian-style stern. While the boat had yet to be fitted out, the captain's bank balance was getting low. Once again, luck and friends intervened. A position was vacant at the French Consulate. Bernard was hired as secretary and for a year became "Monsieur le Chancelier," with a corresponding salary. The rig, the hardware, and all the finishing touches could now be undertaken.

The adventure could continue, with a renewed chance of success. Bernard had improved his knowledge of celestial navigation and he now owned a good Omega watch that enabled him to make an exact position fix. He set sail for South Africa.

The Mozambique Channel is always touch and go and it didn't spare Moitessier. The sea was still rough after a gale when a rogue wave suddenly reared up. It rolled the ketch, putting the masts in the water and Moitessier was swept overboard. As the boat righted itself, he swam frantically back to it. Clambering aboard, he noticed that the cabin hatch, essential to the boat's security, had disappeared. He saw it floating twenty yards away and immediately plunged into the roiling seas and recovered it.

For two years, first in Durban and then in Cape Town, he took on odd jobs to survive, to take care of MARIE-THÉRÈSE II, and to provision for his next voyage. He worked as a shipwright and as a welder, and he developed a technique for caulking under water. He ate cormorants he killed with his slingshot.

During this period, he met Henry Wakelam, a do-it-yourself genius, who had also built his own boat. The two sea vagabonds became inseparable. They would go through trash cans looking for anything they could put to use on board. They were constantly hungry and were extremely creative in finding ways to feed themselves. They crossed the Atlantic together. A novel piece of equipment—self-steering gear—had made it much easier for them to sail their boats. This device, which would become a solo sailor's most precious companion, had been invented by a Frenchman, Marin Marie. A British magazine had published a drawing: a wind vane set at an angle to the wind and connected to a trim tab on the boat's rudder kept the boat on a course relative to the wind direction. A similar contraption adapted by Henry Wakelam, a master of all things practical, was put on MARIE-THÉRÈSE II. It worked. From then on, Moitessier was relieved of having to stay constantly at the helm. *"MARIE-THÉRÈSE II held on alone towards the open sea, making three knots under full sail, with the automatic steering working wonderfully."*[4] This was a wonderful thing, the idea of a trouble-free passage. Nevertheless it didn't herald the complete freedom he'd hoped for.

The maintenance of a wooden boat, built quickly, was a full-time job. In Saint Helena, the ketch was craned onto the quay where, with the help of the trusty Wakelam, Moitessier replaced some rotten planks. He also made a repair at the masthead. By a lucky coincidence, two French naval vessels, JEANNE D'ARC and LA GRANDIÈRE put in at Jamestown. Moitessier enjoyed their warm hospitality and their food. More important, the sailors were very generous with charts they had in duplicate, and with tracing paper so he could copy others lacking on board MARIE-THÉRÈSE II. The officers gave him lessons in astro-navigation, and the medical officer gave useful advice as well as medicine to complement his bare supplies.

A series of passages and ports-of-call then followed, in company with Henry Wakelam's WANDA: Ascension Island, where the skippers fed on birds' eggs and received huge cans of corned beef from the American base; Fernando de Noronha, a tiny island off Brazil; Trinidad; and finally Martinique. Then for the second time, Bernard fell asleep and was shipwrecked.

MARIE-THÉRÈSE II was pillaged at St. Vincent. All Moitessier recovered was an old rusty sea chest containing his meager possessions. He gave his sight reduction tables and his sextant to the skipper of the schooner that took him to Trinidad, and showed him how to use them to calculate latitude. He realized that he would stay poor if he remained in the West Indies. He had to go back to France. "The country is rotten with money," Adolfo, a friend who put him up, told him. "If you write a book, I bet you'll be off in another boat within five years." Moitessier was skeptical: *I had no intention whatever of writing a book, thinking that one had to be very gifted to be able to write.*[5]

An opportunity to return to Europe soon presented itself. Hired on a Norwegian tanker, Bernard made several roundtrip voyages between New York and Trinidad. He was well fed and worked at odd jobs consisting mainly of scraping and painting. *"I learned that the topsides of a ship do not rust if they are maintained in the time-honored manner of the merchant navy: paint, paint, and paint again."* He concluded: *"I started to realize that a properly built steel yacht could be maintained by a well-trained monkey."*[6] He improved his knowledge of celestial navigation: *"The second officer and a young pilot who had taken a liking to me helped me penetrate the secrets of the night sky, the laws of the stars, the planets and the moon."*[7]

When the vessel reached Hamburg, Bernard, with a few dollars in his pocket, jumped on a train to Paris.

Except for a bicycle tour after the war, he had never lived in France. His country was Indochina. His universe was the tropics, the sun, and the sea. He had a rude awakening. *"I was almost thirty-four, with half my life already behind me, and I was starting from scratch with no money, no degree and no skills.* "[8] He looked for work without success, for in 1958 there was a recession. "Paris was a great desert: garrets, and sandwiches." But again luck intervened:

> *Then a patch of blue sky suddenly appeared among the dark clouds: a dream job, a real coat-and-tie affair. Choosing to overlook my somewhat unusual resume, the Midi drug company hired me as a salesman. So the grasshopper would have something to eat and might get through the winter without freezing to death after all. Then, two weeks later, as I was pitching an article in* Le Yacht *magazine, I came across a journalist named Jean-Michel Barrault.*[9]

I must at this point introduce myself, not to brag, but to explain the warm relationship on which I then embarked with Bernard and which lasted 36 years, until his death. Since childhood, I have been in love with sailing. My wife Dany and I had just bought a used 30-foot sailboat. We did a lot of coastal sailing and hoped to one day realize our dream of sailing around the world.

I wrote for the weekly *Le Yacht*. I was in the magazine's offices when a tall, thin guy in a crumpled suit showed up. I was immediately fascinated by this character and by his life as a vagabond on the high seas. I also quickly perceived his distress—in Paris he felt like a stray dog. I invited him to come to my house where he would always be welcome and made to feel at home.

I was very touched to read this page in *Tamata and the Alliance* about this period in his life and me.

> *A series of teachers and guides have appeared at key turning points in my life . . . and now I could thank the skies of Paris for sending me Jean-Michel.*
>
> *"Write a book," he said.*
>
> *"Are you kidding? I am no writer. And besides, having had two shipwrecks does not exactly qualify me to write a book; people would die laughing."*
>
> *"First, you've got a lot more in you than your two shipwrecks. Just write down the stuff you've been telling Dany and me, it'll be terrific. In any case you don't have any choice. Do you really think you'll be able to buy yourself a boat in less than 10 or 15 years of dragging your sample case from one doctor to another? Just write about the wide-open spaces you've known. And if I think you're really working at it, I'll be able to lend you a hand."*
>
> *Until I met Jean-Michel I had been wandering in a kind of fog, trying to forget the caress of the tropical sun and breezes on my bare skin. Then "luck" put him on my path. He took me by the hand, shook me up, opened my eyes. And I saw that life was beautiful and gave it a smile.*[10]

Bernard cleverly scheduled his sales calls to give himself free time, which he would spend tucked away in bistros filling a notebook with his even handwriting. Almost every day, he came to show me what he had written. His talent was apparent. My wife and I needed to give him little more advice than to cut a sentence here, rewrite another, or flesh out a story. At home, our three children, who were then six, five, and four, listened raptly to Uncle Bernard's tales.

At the same time, he was discovering the magic of writing. Flammarion was the French publisher of a series *L'aventure vécue* (True adventures) which included many books written by sailors: Le Toumelin, Annie Van de Wiele, Marcel Bardiaux. Bernard was offered a contract. The director was René d'Uckermann, and the editor in charge of Bernard's manuscript was Parisot. The relationship between writer and editor was not always peaceful. Moitessier complained to Flammarion:

> René d'Uckermann informs me that my manuscript should be reduced by one third. If this is done, what will be left of my book? A skeleton! By cutting too much, we run the risk of losing its amusing and humorous character, as well as the description of the hobo life in port. If we cut the practical sections, nothing much will be left for the interested reader. I hope to have convinced you not to cut too much, and I beg you to forgive me for pretending to teach you your job.

Bernard sent me a copy of the letter, begging me to intervene: "Wouldn't it help if you called Parisot and told him that his idea of cutting some parts will diminish the quality of the book?"

Such is the eternal tug of war between author and editor!

In the meantime, Moitessier moved to the south of France. His parents had left Indochina and were building a house in

Les Lecques, near Marseille. Deshumeurs, repatriated, had gotten involved in rose growing. Bernard held various jobs, some better paying than others, while he continued work on *Sailing to the Reefs*, which wasn't without its setbacks. The release of a second volume of Marcel Bardiaux's story had forced a postponement to Bernard's book, and he resorted to sending registered letters to Flammarion.

Finally in February 1960, the book came out. Bernard, as any new author would, gazed through bookstore windows at the colored picture on the cover of his beloved junk MARIE-THÉRÈSE in the Gulf of Siam. The stubborn sailor was already dreaming, if the book sold well, of MARIE-THÉRÈSE III.

1, 8, 9, 10. *Tamata and the Alliance.*
2, 3, 4. *Sailing to the Reefs.*
5, 6, 7. *Cape Horn: the logical route.*

5

From MAÏTE *to* JOSHUA

Moitessier took advantage of his travels around the south of France as a salesman for various firms to visit bookstores and hold signing sessions, which were well attended. He was invited to talk on a prestigious literary show *Lectures pour tous* (Readings for all). He came over as amiable and convincing. The book sold well, the readers liked it, and Bernard made himself important new friends. One of them wrote to him: "I loved your book. I am an amateur naval architect and since you will need a new boat, I am offering to draw the plans, free of charge of course."

The letter was from Jean Knocker, a horticulturist by trade who had designed several sailboats, including CASARCA, a cold-molded wooden ketch for his son-in-law, Pierre Jeanson. Pierre loved to sail and was as generous as his father-in-law. One of their partners in the family business was Henri Brun, a gifted handyman who invented an ingenious wind vane. Marketed as the Atoms, it became a great hit with sailors.

Bernard wrote to me in April 1960. "I sent a letter to Knocker who has kindly offered to draw the plans for MAÏTE."

The architect and the sailor exchanged numerous letters. Although Bernard was not yet able to fund his boat, Jean Knocker wanted to get started. In letter after letter, the sailor outlined what he had in mind.

March 22, 1960

For the moment I cannot think too much about MAÏTE. It would cost an astronomical sum. I must be patient, very patient . . . Right now, I just have to work hard. Then we will see. If you want a general idea, I'm thinking of a Tahiti ketch . . . All of this belongs to a dream world. I could be seduced by anything.

April 19, 1960

I am very touched by your understanding about whether or not we should discuss my future boat. In a way, it's best to talk about it, though we cannot do much at this point.

Bernard developed in great detail several of his ideas and doubts, the pros and cons of a center cockpit, the characteristics of a double-ender, and the properties of cold-molded construction among them. He started thinking about building in steel, which is so much tougher than wood. In a letter dated May 19, he wrote: "You're right. Since I'm going to get a boat anyway, I might as well think about it now and follow your advice."

He set down the dimensions he wanted:

LOA: 31' 3"

Beam: 10' 6"

Draft: 4' 4"

She was to be a Marconi ketch, double-ended, and full at the waterline.

He agreed that cold-molded construction would be easy to build but at the same time praised the qualities of steel. He insisted on comfort:

Steel or iron construction is much more solid than wood. What would be ideal for me is an iron hull that I could buy bare. I would fit it out by myself, bit by bit, doing everything with my own hands. Regarding accommodations, another idea might be an aft cabin, in case one day I have children . . . My dear friend, you see where we are heading! Nowhere for the moment. Design MAÏTE, the two of us? It doesn't seem to make too much sense for now.

On May 21, he wrote to the architect: "We won't start building for another year." Four days later, he sent me this note: "I have made up my mind: I will build the boat myself in Marseille in cold-molded wood so it'll be perfectly watertight, totally rigid, and easy to build, and I can cover it with three layers of fiberglass."

In his letters to Knocker, which were becoming more and more frequent, Bernard seemed very excited, as if he could see the light at the end of the tunnel and was running toward it.

Marseille, June 2, 1960

Thank you for your letter. I can already smell the sea and the islands. But before you take your pencil again, we will have to change the dimensions (I do apologize):

Length: 34' 6"

Beam: 10' 6" to 11'

Draft: 4' 4" to 4' 6"

Cabin headroom: 6' (that point was underlined twice with red ink)

Bernard was thinking of having a small motor installed, even though he'd never had one before. And he was becoming very impatient. Now hoping to get started in the fall, he contacted Gaubert, a shipyard that specialized in cold-molded construction. He drew plans and submitted them to the architect, showing him his ideas and marking the most important ones in red ink. He was already thinking of long voyages. "<u>Berths</u>: you have no idea how important it is to have wide berths and a narrow sole for this type of sailing. It is unbelievable how much usable volume can be gained with a <u>narrow sole</u> on the plan . . . It's best to keep it simple if I want to go back to sea!"

He wished for "a large metal or polyester container to keep dry a large amount of rice, lentils, and split peas. It's very important when you carry your house with you to be able to do the provisioning cheaply. In Saint Helena, Wakelam and I missed out on buying cheaply ten additional five-gallon containers of dry milk that we would have exchanged for corned beef."

To satisfy his constant need to be at sea, Bernard jumped at the chance to sail in the Giraglia regatta on a Sergent 36. He called it "a nice outing despite the perils of the Mediterranean. Racing in sailboats there is like playing poker." In the meantime, he had received the plans from Knocker, with the modifications he'd requested.

Marseille, September 15, 1960

I'm returning to you the copies of the plan. They are beautiful and I couldn't resist showing them to Mauric, the architect, whom I've met. Mauric thinks it is one of the best plans for a Norwegian-style ketch he has ever seen . . . I will be in Paris early October for the Boat Show. After the show, I would like Jouët to hire me as an apprentice for one month in his boatyard to learn about cold-molded construction. After this, could I stay with you for one or two weeks if I can be of any use for the boat plans? At the same time, I could help your agricultural workers to rake the soil or push wheelbarrows filled with fertilizer. It would keep me in good physical as well as mental shape.

He didn't stay with Knocker because he had to rush back to the south of France to take up a job that promised to be a goldmine. It involved selling to garages containers of wax polish that would give autos a beautiful luster. As his demonstration showed, by rubbing a small area vigorously, you got a spectacular result. However, doing the whole car was a labor of a different order. He developed a technique. In each town, he would call on the largest garage, make his sales pitch in a German accent, and leave a free sample. He would fill out an order form "Left a can as a sample," and would then put the garage's stamp on two more forms that he kept. He would then create a fake order for 15 cans, made authentic by the stamp, and show it to the other garage owners who, not wanting to miss out, would also order. The traveling salesman beat a path around the south of France.

Castelnaudary, December 16, 1960

I'm doing very well. But this is hard work. Nevertheless in six weeks, I've already paid for the 3-ton keel.

Two days later, he wrote to us optimistically:

I hope to have enough money to get the boat started April or May. Right now, I'm driving around, but I sent a check to the wood supplier (a hefty sum just for the 3mm wood planking). It's freezing on the road, but the thought that every customer helps to pay for the boat warms me up . . . And now, one minute of silence and don't say a word: I'm getting married in a few days.

Françoise was a medical technician in the field of electro-encephalography. Her parents and Bernard's were old friends—

their fathers had attended the same high school in Marseille. It was only to be expected that while he was doing the rounds of the Midi, Bernard would run into her again. In her book, *60,000 Milles à la Voile (60,000 Miles under Sail)*, Françoise wrote: "Bernard left, came back, left again, and we always enjoyed meeting again. My children adored him." Two years passed. Then Françoise received a good job offer in Brussels. Bernard didn't want her to go and suggested getting married. *"We will add a berth to the boat, a wedding to our lives."*[1]

They were married on December 24, 1960. How could he who had broken off his engagement in Indochina with Marie-Thérèse, whom he adored, now give up his independence? Françoise had married very young, and her first experience was a failure. The mother of three children, she had to learn a trade to survive. Even if she was under the spell of this supersensitive poet who could open the door to adventure, she must have been aware of all the pitfalls. Perhaps, like many sailors' wives before her, she hoped to change him. There's no doubt she expected to play an important role for him. *"Bernard is very complicated. He needs to be reassured. More instinct than reason, he is unpredictable."*[2]

On the eve of the wedding, both had cold feet and they spent all night talking. At 6 a.m., the outcome was negative. At 10 a.m. Bernard got Françoise out of the shower. The wedding was on. Their friends were waiting. Bernard was in love. *"An extraordinary little woman: apart from possessing all the necessary qualities that make an ideal wife, Françoise had answered in a single stroke all the questions that bedevil families by presenting me with three children by a previous marriage."*[3]

Françoise's three children were the same age as ours. When he announced his wedding, Bernard told us, "She has three children, like you do." Was the vagabond ready to settle down? He admitted as much, *"So here I am at last with a complete family, all the lost time made up for. If this isn't perfect bliss: sitting by the fireplace, in slippers . . ."*[4] As if the sea bird could find happiness in a cage, however comfortable it might be!

The plans for a boat remained alive. The letters between the sailor and the naval architect were becoming more and more numerous and friendlier with time. By the beginning of 1961, the relationship between Bernard and Knocker was less formal, "Dear Sir" had been replaced by "Dear friend." Bernard politely sent his greetings to Knocker's wife.

He extended his sales calls to Bordeaux, where the garage owners "were nice enough to contribute to half of the future Dacron sails." He continued to insist on an aft cabin, which would make the chartering he had in mind a little easier.

> The customers realize very quickly that being in port (with hotels nearby) is much more pleasant than being offshore . . . MAÏTE will mainly sail in the West Indies and the Pacific, with Françoise and me on board, and to earn some money, we will have a good camera, paper, and a typewriter. Then the aft cabin will become a necessity, as I will be able to isolate myself to work (!), think (!), and also to enjoy our married life.

The exchange of letters continued during the early months of 1961, with a plan for the keel casting, and construction expected to begin in the fall. Selling his cans was still hard graft, but lucrative. Suddenly, everything changed:

Chauffailles, June 29, 1961

I am afraid this letter will disappoint you after all the trouble you've taken to create a beautiful plan.

1. I will start building my boat in September.
2. It will be in steel.
3. The length will be 39 feet 6 inches.
4. It will be built according to your plan enlarged by 1/5.

Don't try to make me change my mind. The owner of an excavator factory who loves boats wrote to me after reading my book and asked me to get in contact with him. We decided on the following:

a. I will sail with him in July-August and will fix his boat. Although he knows little about sailing he has a fine steel boat, expertly built by the workers in his factory.
b. He will start working on my boat on September 1 and will build the hull decked and fitted with the two cabin-trunks for the total price of 700,000 francs, including transportation by truck to Lyon and launching it there. I will be involved in the construction and will work with two of his workers.

I made some inquiries. Jean Fricaud is reliable and can be trusted. He's helping me because he likes me and also

because he would like some day to build steel boats. The
hull must be finished in three months.

Moitessier had been thinking of building in cold-molded
wood because it's easy to work with, but he was fully aware of
steel's greater strength. When arriving in Hamburg on the Norwegian tanker, he had witnessed a steel lifeboat being crushed
between the tanker and the quay. It was repaired; the hull was
jacked out and the holes filled with rivets. Under the same circumstances a wooden boat would have been reduced to splin-
ters. Even if he vowed to be more careful on his future cruises,
he might anyway find himself in a situation that a steel hull
would better survive. He enthusiastically accepted Fricaud's
offer to charge only for the material. He would be able to use
knowledge he'd acquired working in Cape Town: *"Noting my
knack for welding, Barlé took me seriously in hand, as some teachers know how to do. With my interest in welding and his excellent
knowledge of it, he had decided to teach it to me thoroughly."*[5]

As Bernard saw the boat of his dreams taking shape, he
made another decision. Now that he was married, it was time
to leave behind the love of his youth. MAÏTE became JOSHUA,
in honor of Joshua Slocum, the first solo circumnavigator.

Before starting to build the boat, Bernard was happily surprised
by a visit from his old friend Henry Wakelam, who proposed
bringing his WANDA to France the next summer. Since Dany and
I were also thinking of building our long-term cruising vessel,

Bernard started dreaming, saying it would be great for all three boats to take off together for the Canary Islands. At the end of August, he wrote to us that he was moving to Chauffailles.

> I'm leaving tomorrow for the yard where the construction of my boat will start. I will team with three other workers. No need to tell you that I'll put in a lot of overtime from day one to get the thing going. I'll challenge the limits of my abilities, both practical (cutting, filing, welding) and mental (tracing each element, changing from 36-foot cold-molded wood to 39-foot steel).

Bernard emphasized the strength of metal. Since we were planning to build, in Holland, a 36-foot double ended ketch quite similar to JOSHUA but made of teak, he suggested: "Throw out of the window of your fifth floor apartment your metal file cabinet and your wooden desk. Then go down to look at the results before the cops arrive. You will be convinced of the superiority of steel!"

In the meantime, at Fricaud's plant, the work was progressing rapidly, to Moitessier's delight. "I'm working 60 hours every week and I'm completely exhausted. We started two months and two days ago. The deck is in place and the sides of the two cabins and the center cockpit are welded."

Early in 1962, the hull was completed and launched in Lyon. JOSHUA reached Marseille on March 2. The hull was bare: no rigging, no motor, no ballast, and no interior furniture—and the first group of sailing school students was due on board on May 1. Moitessier started working furiously, first because he had to hurry but also because he wanted to get back to sea. At the same time he was proving that if you really wanted to go sailing, there was no need to wait until the boat was fully equipped. He had learned a lot from the fishermen in the Gulf of Siam.

On March 25, he wrote to Jean Knocker:

> The mainmast is finished: a 57-foot telegraph pole. It's heavy but I don't have a choice for this summer. The same goes for the mizzen. The main cabin is almost done with lots of storage lockers. The forepeak is almost finished. What remains are the galley, the chart table, and the aft cabin. Everything must be ready for trials by April 15. Instead of the motor, we will have four solid oars.

Friends lent a helping hand. Best of all was the appearance of Henry Wakelam. He had sailed WANDA to England, married Ann, and now came to join his old friend in France. A friend of Moitessier gave him a small two-stroke 7-hp motor. Within 10 days, the talented Wakelam contrived to install the motor, including the shaft and propeller—without hauling the boat. The boat was fitted out at a crazy pace. Henry demonstrated once more, as he had in Durban and Cape Town, his ingenuity, which included rummaging through the garbage. In a trashcan at the club in Cape Town, he had found some lengths of used nylon line discarded by the whaling ships. By recycling the still usable strands, Henry and Bernard had made themselves halyards, sheets, and mooring warps.

Françoise and Ann sewed sleeping bags, curtains, and cushions. Bernard spliced sheets and halyards. The shrouds were made of galvanized wire from the phone company. The sails were fitted with rows of reef points. JOSHUA would get by without a large genoa. Instead of a storm jib, a set of reef points in the jib would do. There were no winches. Instead, there was a portable, multi-purpose, block and tackle named *Attila*. In two and a half months, the small team had managed to turn a bare hull into a sailboat ready to put to sea, even if there was a good chance that, here and there, a temporary fitting would become a fixture. As Bernard said, *"the main thing is that we're covering miles instead of wasting time installing gadgets that cost a fortune and aren't needed for the time being."*[6]

Three years after the shipwreck that left him in despair on a rock in the West Indies, Moitessier had written a successful book, was married with three beautiful stepchildren, and was at the helm of a somewhat primitive but solid 40-foot steel ketch. All the oceans of the world now beckoned.

1, 2. *60,000 Milles à la Voile.*
3, 4. *Cape Horn: the logical route.*
5. *Sailing to the Reefs.*
6. *Tamata and the Alliance.*

6

A honeymoon
around the world

All the world's oceans beckoned, but not right away. Bernard
had promised Françoise the greatest trip for their honeymoon—the West Indies and the Pacific—but they still needed
a full kitty. Instead of chartering, as he had thought of doing,
Moitessier decided to embark a crew of sailing-school students.
Sailing between Marseille, Toulon, and Corsica, he taught them
skills outside the usual curriculum. He had never forgotten
what Phuoc's father had said when he returned his compass, a
gift both magical and treacherous: *You need light to use this
thing at night and that blinds you.*[1]

Bernard told his crew to forget the instruments, to sail not
with their eyes fixed on the compass but by choosing a star to
steer by. He taught his students to use all their senses, to feel

the caress of the breeze on their skin and the movement of the boat on their body, and to sense where the swell was coming from and its amplitude. At night, black rags in the shrouds show the wind's direction and are more visible in the darkness. The approach of land is revealed by the smell of grass, or by watching the flight of a bird. All maneuvers were carried out under sail, and the crew learned how to sail the boat backwards by backing the staysail and the mizzen. Teaching was a two-way street: *"I can also thank my crews, because a master's teaching benefits not only his disciples but also the master himself. Each person brings some scrap of knowledge that feeds the entire group."*[2] At the same time, Moitessier wrote articles for *Bateaux* magazine in which he described his techniques and offered tips, which were largely original.

The season came to an end. The skipper was exhausted, and so was Françoise who, on top of her jobs in clinics and hospitals, was helping to run the sailing school. Winter was on its way. The Pacific with its sunshine, its atolls, and its crystal waters was becoming more and more appealing. They spent their evenings in conversation with Henry and Ann, who'd fixed up an old wreck that had sunk in Port-Miou, and the Merlots, whom Bernard had met in Durban and who'd just bought a splendid 50-foot sailboat in Cannes.

Before they could leave, they had to figure out what to do with the children. Béatrice, the oldest, was 12, and the boys, Emmanuel and Hervé, 11 and 10. The boys would go to a boarding school and Béatrice would stay with Françoise's sister. Françoise was sad to be leaving them and Bernard promised that they wouldn't stay away too long. The Merlots had spoken highly of the Red Sea. Françoise begged: *"Bernard, we will come back by way of the Red Sea, won't we? We will get to see the children earlier that way."*[3]

After a second season of sailing school, which brought its own share of new experiences, everything was ready. JOSHUA was in perfect order. The kitty was flush. Françoise arranged her leave and rented her apartment. The newly-weds had even bought a piece of land where they might one day build a house. The vagabond already saw the future in a different light:

> *Sail on and on until I've had my fill of it . . . drop the hook awhile, once I'm drunk on salt spray . . . write a second book, then do a few more seasons of cruising school . . . and then, a very long time in the future, a very, very long time, when I'm all wrinkled and preserved by salt, quietly spend my old age with a spade in my hand in a nice garden, close to a simple cabin with Françoise inside.*[4]

It was an enchanting vision, while in the back of his mind the thought always remained that JOSHUA would be there when-ever he wanted to leave. The vagabond, perhaps, wanted to set down roots at the very moment he'd attained what Deshumeurs fondly called "escape velocity," that sent you in orbit *"where you cruise so high that life can never again shoot you down."*[5]

On the face of it, Moitessier had every reason to be happy. What was missing? What absolute truth was he searching for? Was the Dragon lying in wait to ambush him? One could sense his angst when he wrote: *"Deep in my gut I knew I had to leave, and fast. Every fiber of my body longed for wide-open spaces . . .*

Make sail and the rest will follow. Return to your beloved tropics, get yourself far from noise, money grubbing, and complications. Once you're in the heart of the trades with your wife and your boat, everything will become crystal clear. "[6]

On October 30, 1963, JOSHUA and her crew left Marseille and, in short hops when the weather forecast was good, made it to Gibraltar and then to Morocco, where they stayed for the winter. Bernard's parents, Robert and Marthe, had left Indochina in 1947. Robert had joined his brother André in Casablanca, Morocco where he acquired the franchise for a German tire company. They lived in a lovely house surrounded by a flower garden. This was the last time that Bernard would see the father who'd masked his love for his children behind a stern exterior. Robert Moitessier died on August 31, 1964 while his eldest son was sailing on the other side of the world. Her husband gone, Marthe left Morocco and settled in Les Lecques.

While in Casablanca, Françoise found a job. The money allowed them to send for Béatrice and they acquired a little mascot, a dog named Youki. Bernard's parents suggested a car trip to the south of the country to visit Safi and Marrakech. After 24 hours, Bernard, concerned for his boat, left his parents and Françoise, who couldn't understand his anxiety, and took the bus back to JOSHUA, all the while safely berthed in Casablanca's harbor.

When they left Casablanca for the Canary Islands, two crew joined them. Loïck Fougeron was an old friend who'd crossed the Atlantic and had done several other deliveries, and Claude Lafon was a dentist who wanted more offshore sailing experience and who proved to be a gifted, reliable crewmember. In a spell of squally weather, Moitessier decided to stay on watch all night. At dawn, Françoise came up, bringing him a cup of coffee and a cigarette. Bernard appreciated her gesture, and called her a rare gem.

They spent the summer in the Canaries, where Béatrice was joined by her two brothers. Aboard JOSHUA, anchored off the marvelous beach at Fuerteventura, the children had a grand time. Everyone was happy.

In France, Eric Tabarly's victory in the 1964 Solo Trans-Atlantic Race was on the front page of all the newspapers and made the cover of every magazine. Bernard wrote to me from Las Palmas:

> Please send me the articles about the race . . . Try to make some noise about England's revenge in four years so that a few good French boats will join the race. There will probably be 30 to 40 boats, several of them equipped by the Queen of England who most likely didn't take Tabarly's victory well. If I'm back with JOSHUA, I'll try to be in it. Marin Marie might be right when he says that a 50-foot boat is not too big for solo racing. It's not physical strength that matters the most but guile. If the English sailors figure that out, we're probably done for.

In the fall, when the children returned to school, a number of "ocean birds" joined them, en route to the tropics: Pierre and Cathy Deshumeurs, Bluche, who with CHIMÈRE had already sailed around the world, and Henry and Ann Wakelam who had refitted a 55-foot steel hull, an abandoned buoy tender that they'd named PHEB after the vessel's former duty of tending *phares et balises* (lights and beacons). They were waiting for Alain Hervé's AVENTURE. Unexpectedly, they were joined by a singlehanded sailor, Pierre Auboiroux, who offset his inexperience with a fetching optimism and who'd managed to cram all the essentials of life into one word: "go."

In his book, *Cape Horn: the Logical Route*, Moitessier has recounted at length and very well the happy passages he made with Françoise. Crossing the Atlantic, the ketch showed how fast she could be, making days' runs of 180 miles. Bernard heard JOSHUA's song: *"Give me wind and I'll give you miles."*[7] Françoise was seduced by a "wake of a million diamonds." Her apprenticeship was ongoing. She was learning how to handle the boat by herself, repair the sails, and take a fix. *"I cannot stop thinking about the children but I am not sad,"*[8] she said.

The circumnavigation had hardly begun and his promise to Françoise—not to stay away from the children for too long—was already creating a dilemma for Bernard. If they wanted to enjoy the islands, get to know the inhabitants, and respect the seasons to avoid hurricanes and cyclones, the circumnavigation would take years. Alternatively, they would have to reduce the number of stops, stay only for short periods of time, and come back feeling they had missed out. *"If we went home by the westward route, as we had planned from the beginning, we would have to tear through the Pacific in order to get through the Torres Straits before the start of the bad season and we might come to hate the Pacific as much as I had hated the Caribbean eight years ago."*[9]

There was another solution: get Béatrice, Emmanuel, and Hervé to come to Polynesia for the summer holidays, or leave the boat in Papeete and go back to France to spend a few months with them there. Unfortunately the cost of the plane tickets was beyond their reach.

A third possibility remained—maybe. While pushed by a fine trade wind, escorted by dolphins, and chasing flying fish, the red ketch ate up the miles, Bernard was deep in thought, turning a small globe in his hands. Françoise saw him looking at it. She was disturbed: "Why are you looking down there? You're not thinking of going home that way?" That way was Cape Horn, the southern route, that of the sailing ships of the past. A few sailors had already been there: Vito Dumas, the Argentinian, solo; O'Brien, the Irish sailor; and Marcel Bardiaux who'd rounded it from east to west.

They would stay briefly in Martinique, Bernard decided. They would come back another time to the West Indies. The dream now was the Pacific islands, the atolls, and the lagoons. *"Just a good scrubbing down, two coats of antifouling and we would be off. We had chosen the Pacific right from the start and we would return quickly by way of the Red Sea. Everything was settled."*[10] But they kept extending their stay. First it was to celebrate Christmas with friends who arrived one after the other. Bernard wrote to us: "Henry is here with Bluche on CHIMÈRE, Blondeau singlehander on double-keeled AIGLE DE MER and another singlehander on NÉO VENT, a 25-foot sloop. It took him 55 days from the Canary Islands to Martinique because there was no self-steering gear on board (and because of the calms this year) . . ."

The Deshumeurs had chosen to go by way of Dakar. Moitessier worried because Alain Hervé's AVENTURE had not arrived yet, but he learned later that they'd only left the Canaries on January 4 and were headed for Barbados.

On December 24 the sea vagabonds had a party on board PHEB, the Wakelams' ketch. Bernard admitted that he was missing the children, and tried to raise a new thought he had.

"Françoise, we'll be back home soon . . . we could even return from Tahiti via Cape Horn."

"You're kidding!"

"Of course!"[11]

Bluche talked about the Smeetons whom he'd met in New Zealand. The Smeetons, a British couple, had wanted to get back home quickly to their daughter and decided to go by way of Cape Horn. Their ketch, TZU-HANG, which was about the same size as JOSHUA, pitchpoled. Beryl Smeeton was at the helm when TZU-HANG capsized and she was thrown overboard. The tether of her safety harness snapped like a thread, but though injured, the tenacious Beryl struggled back to the boat. TZU-HANG was dismasted and, with her deck stove in, was near to sinking. After reaching Chile under jury rig, TZU-HANG set out a second time and was again knocked down and dismasted. Miles Smeeton told their story in the book *Once is Enough*.

Bernard was still tempted to return by way of Cape Horn, even though he didn't dare mention it again. It would be a logical route, allowing them to spend some time in the Pacific and then return quickly to Europe.

Moitessier was inclined to linger unnecessarily long wherever he stopped. Once before, in Singapore, a late departure had forced him to face the contrary season. Again in Fort-de-France, their stay dragged on for no good reason. During a two-month layover, they'd not seen anything else of the West Indies. Finally on February 14, JOSHUA left Martinique for Panama. Driven smartly along by a beautiful fresh trade wind, she covered the 1,224 miles in seven days and 14 hours. Françoise too, Bernard said, heard JOSHUA murmur: "Give me wind, I shall give you miles." The transit of the Panama Canal was uneventful. And now what? *If we had wanted to return by way of Torres Straits we would have had one long rush . . . One look at the globe, though, will reveal that the distance is the same via Cape Horn, with one important difference: one can be home in four or five months.*[12]

Bernard pretended to hesitate, but he'd made up his mind. A friend had lent him a copy of *Once is Enough*. He'd studied the reasons for TZU-HANG's dismastings, and read Smeeton's analyses and advice. He knew he would gain from the experience of the sailors who had preceded him. The American Hydrographic Service in Panama had given him charts of Tierra del Fuego. He told Françoise: *I have already lost two boats, I don't want to lose this one. Now, we will take JOSHUA by the route which I consider the safest, the most logical. On board JOSHUA I am first of all the skipper.*[13]

Françoise was nervous. "The more I looked into it, the more the logical route seemed to me the one at 30,000 feet above sea level aboard a comfortable Air France jet." Bernard offered her a plane ticket, but courageously she said no. *"You have decided to round Cape Horn and with or without me, you will do it. We left France together and we will return together, regardless of the chosen route."*[14]

It's possible Moitessier's decision was influenced by an odd incident in the past. Shortly after *Sailing to the Reefs* was published and the building of a new boat seemed far into the future, Deshumeurs had recommended Bernard visit a woman in Antibes, a psychic. To consult a fortune-teller was hardly Deshumeurs's style, less so Bernard's. But some months later, finding himself in town with a free afternoon, Bernard climbed the stairs to the fortune-teller's place. "I was dressed like any traveling salesman, my hands hadn't coiled a line in ages," he wrote. The woman spread out her cards, stared at them, and gathered them three times. *"She sat still for a long time, as if fascinated. And then she started to speak, in a steady stream: 'water . . . a lot of water . . . lots and lots of water'."*[15] JOSHUA had whispered the same refrain in the Atlantic and the Caribbean Sea.

To round Cape Horn during the Southern Hemisphere summer, the favorable season, they would have to set sail in November from Tahiti. That would bring them back to Europe for Easter 1966. They had quite a few months to enjoy the marvelous harbors the Pacific islands promised them.

───── ∞ ─────

In the days of the sailing ships, captains feared the passage from Panama to the Galápagos which was bedeviled by dead calms, erratic currents, and fair-weather mists that would cause an island visible in the evening to disappear the next day. Because of these mysterious happenings, the Galápagos were called the "Enchanted Archipelago." Taking advantage of a steady wind, JOSHUA made the 1,000 mile passage in nine days. For 30 dollars, Bernard and Françoise were able to secure a visa from the Ecuadorian Consul in Panama which allowed them to visit the archipelago. This is no longer the case for yachts which can now stay only a few days at anchor in Wreck Bay and Academy Bay. If the crews wish to visit other islands, they have to go on a tour boat or take a guide on board.

JOSHUA's crew was able to anchor north of Barrington Island in the limpid water of a small lagoon. The scenery was both beautiful and austere. They found perfect shelter between the main island that was deserted, dry, rocky, and covered with giant cacti where iguanas dozed and a rocky islet that ended in a causeway. At the end of the lagoon, hundreds of seals lounged on two white sandy beaches.

In 1981, I anchored stealthily in this marvelous spot, only to be found by officials who ordered me to leave immediately, under threat of a fine or jail. But the Moitessiers were able to stay for six weeks in this world where creatures knew no fear. They played in the water with the seals, caught enormous morays, and captured turtles to eat and to preserve their meat. At the same time, they painted the topsides and simply enjoyed being in this deserted anchorage at an island close to the origins of the universe.

JOSHUA had a magnificent passage after leaving the Galápagos: 3,000 miles in the trade winds, with no threat from reefs or bad weather. The ketch was in perfect condition. Taking advantage of a big tide, they had careened the boat in a rocky cleft in Academy Bay, cleaned the bottom, and coated it with antifouling. Pushed by a nice breeze, JOSHUA covered half the distance in nine days with two 24-hour runs of 187 and 192 miles. The skipper liked to perch on the pulpit where he could hear the bow sing its song . . . *I shall give you miles . . . thousands of miles.* It seemed that Bernard, calmed by the peacefulness of Barrington and the joy of sailing, had shed the anxiousness he'd shown before leaving Marseille. *"I felt utterly at peace with myself, with Françoise, with my boat."*[16] He was now convinced he'd made the right decision. *"It would all be justified, and besides we would have the most exciting sailing a mariner could dream of . . . the most beautiful for a boat like JOSHUA sailing close-reefed along the way the old sailing ships used to take when they returned home by the shortest route."*[17]

The Marquesas satisfied all the Moitessiers' dreams of the Pacific. In Hiva Oa they spent every evening sitting next to a couple of Marquesians, helping them grate coconut and pound coffee. Bernard was reminded of his childhood. *"Memories of my native Indochina were brought back to life by this big mango tree."*[18] On Fatu Hiva, the beautiful bay of Hanavavé enchanted them, as it has everyone who ever arrived there on a sailboat: *"Neither Françoise nor I had ever beheld scenery which combined in such a compact way all the elements of utter beauty."*[19] They joined in the life of the village and celebrated Bastille Day. Bernard entered a swimming race and won.

In every anchorage, at dawn and dusk, Bernard took out his sextant and took star sights. He had discovered the "both eyes open" technique and the best way to position a star on the horizon. These observations can only be taken in a 10-minute period each morning and evening, when the planets, the stars, and the horizon are all visible. This was a difficult exercise from the deck of a small sailboat at sea, yet in a time long before the invention of GPS, only a good star sight would guarantee them a safe landfall on the Tuamotus, known as the "dangerous archipelago" because of the numerous shipwrecks in their waters.

⊶⊷

Coral rings visible from only a few miles away, the Tuamotus with their treacherous currents and no navigation marks are a sailor's nightmare. Le Toumelin, a famous French sailor who circumnavigated in the early 1950s and wrote about it in KURUN *Around the World 1949-1952*, didn't risk putting in there, despite having a crewmember on board. In his book, he wrote about the atoll of Ahé, which has one of the easiest entrances in the archipelago: "Arriving off the pass, I almost went in the lagoon . . . but I had made up my mind to go directly to Tahiti." Alain Gerbault who sailed around the world in 1923 on FIRECREST was less prudent. "The currents were dangerous and uncertain, the charts often wrong. This seemed an interesting challenge." Nearing Raroia's atoll, he was seduced by the bluish transparency of the air, the delicate colors of the sky over the waters of the lagoon. To get through the pass, Gerbault had to negotiate a strong current that almost made his cutter spin out of control.

Bernard also wanted to experience first hand these magical

lagoons. The vagabond who'd left Indochina on his junk, trusting his instincts when he had no navigation instruments, had changed a lot. He and his rugged steel ketch no longer needed to estimate and to approximate: He was a married man, providing for his family; he now owned a seaworthy vessel; he had a thorough knowledge of celestial navigation; he had practiced exercises and star sights at length; he could fix his position to within a mile.

He prepared with utmost care the 420-mile passage to Takaroa, their first stop in the Tuamotus. The pass into the lagoon is not the easiest. The long entrance channel runs in a straight line, fringed with coral on both sides. Opposite the village, to port, was a quay where boats could go alongside. But with its strong current and undertow, the pass should only be attempted in good weather. Even then, it leads to what appears to be a dead end. Bernard had been swayed in his choice by reading Bluche's description in his book, *The Voyage of CHIMÈRE:* "Everything was easy until we got to the end, the spot where it turns to the left at a right-angle. The current there is fierce and causes strong eddies."

At low-tide slack, JOSHUA hove to off the pass. *"It opened like a funnel in the reef, with the quay on the left, then it continued almost straight, very long (300 yards perhaps) like a green trench cut through the brown of the reefs just above water level."*[20] Everything was ready. But Moitessier hesitated. *"The channel acted like a magnet, we had to enter it while the tide was slack . . . or tear ourselves away quickly and roll about out to sea."* Impeccable boat handling got them in: *"Pure sailing . . . this light shining round the boat . . . these tremendous electrical discharges which surge through your vitals and guide you on without releasing you until you emerge in the blue and green lagoon with this feeling of absolute perfection. It was the finest experience in the whole of my sailing career.*"[21]

Reaching the calm of the lagoon, they anchored in perfect shelter, surrounded by shoals of fish, sea urchins, lobsters, and the breathtaking beauty of the coral depths. "We could have stayed a year without getting bored."

Bernard remembered this happiness he had known in Polynesia when, turning his back on Europe, he decided: *"I am continuing toward the islands of the Pacific."*

1, 2, 4, 5, 6, 15. *Tamata and the Alliance.*
3, 7, 9, 10, 11, 12, 13, 16, 17, 18, 19, 20, 21. *Cape Horn: the logical route.*
8, 14. 60,000 *Milles à la Voile.*

7

Cape Horn

On August 18, 1965, JOSHUA anchored in Papeete Harbor. The Moitessiers spent three months preparing the ketch for the Southern Ocean. Bernard had told us of his plan but asked us to keep quiet about it. In a letter dated September 5, he wrote about the beauty of the Galápagos, the Marquesas, and Takaroa.

> Absolutely marvelous, sea urchins as big as small co-conuts, with quills as big as pencils . . . With ten of them, you have a full meal. We also caught a few lobsters . . . We'll head back to France by the shortest way, eastward, taking advantage of the southern summer. Françoise is not terribly enthusiastic about Cape Horn . . . In the

meantime I'm keeping busy checking the rigging, and doubling the halyards of all the sails . . . Let's hope the summer is not too bad in the south.

Had Bernard ever told Françoise about the fortune-teller who in a trance had seen "water, lots of water"? She had affirmed that she saw neither death nor misfortune in the swirling liquid. Bernard tried to reassure us.

> Don't worry too much about our next leg. Since reading *Once is Enough* I've been taking meticulous care of JOSHUA. I'm building a large sea anchor with mooring swivels, beefing up the rigging and attending to all the details. We're not going to go through the Magellan Strait since the entrance would be a big problem in poor visibility. We'll be better off staying offshore rather than trying to make a pinpoint landfall on the Strait. I'm a whiz at celestial navigation.

Running backstays were added to counter the load on the staysail stay in heavy weather, the stanchions were raised, and the small pulpit on the bowsprit was strengthened. But the main improvement was the installation of an inside steering position. A simple household tin basin was bolted to the cabin roof hatch, forming a dome. With five tiny rectangular Plexiglas windows, this cupola would allow them to steer from a gimbaled seat Bernard had rigged near the inside wheel.

Moitessier had talked to W.A. Robinson about his attempt to round Cape Horn on VARUA. After a storm during which this 70-foot schooner would take off on 100-yard surfs, burying the bowsprit under water, he'd decided to head back to Tahiti. In the epilog of *Once is Enough*, Smeeton, drawing the consequences of what happened on his voyage, wrote: *"It is certain that other yachts will try it. Some will be successful and some like us will fail. It isn't a trip to be undertaken lightly, however good the ship . . . there are gales and seas, particularly in the higher latitudes, which a ship may sometimes meet with, which she will be lucky to survive whatever she does."*

Reflecting on the tactics to use in heavy weather, he had this to say: *"The answer seems to be to keep forty-foot ships out of forty-foot seas, but if forced to run before them to tow long enough lines so that there is an effective drag in spite of the forward movement of the water on the crest."*[1]

Following this advice, Bernard took on board everything he might need to slow the boat down under bare poles: a heavy net used to hoist cargo from the hold of a ship was turned into a sea anchor. Five other trailing lines were readied: three of them hemp, each weighed down by two 40-pound iron pigs, one would tow the sea anchor, and the last was a 300-foot nylon warp. All five lines were coiled in the aft cabin, ready to be used when needed. Françoise put aboard provisioning for six months, much of it stored in watertight lockers. Thanks to the French Navy, the ketch had been hauled out and the bottom scrubbed. Bernard was delighted to find no trace of electrolysis on the hull. On October 21, he sent us the following letter:

Don't worry, we will be very careful. I think I've done all I possibly can. I worked like a dog so JOSHUA can do honor to its namesake. We're thinking of maybe stopping at Saint Helena, or the Azores, but I would like to visit Buenos Aires and Rio.

Jacques Arthaud, who owned a publishing house, had about that time asked me to be the editor for a series of books on the sea and I'd suggested to Moitessier that we would publish his next book. "If I write it one day, we will decide on the publisher. Thanks for your offer, we might talk about it again."

While waiting for the appropriate time to leave Polynesia and reach the forties and fifties during the austral summer, JOSHUA's crew left Papeete to find peace and quiet in Moorea, Tahiti's pretty little sister. While in Cook Bay for 10 days, moored to a pontoon, JOSHUA received some finishing touches. Bernard added patches on the sails in areas where they might chafe, removed the propeller, and dived on the hull to give it a final scrubbing. Finally, on November 23, in a fair breeze, JOSHUA left the bay and turned south.

Weeks turned into months in which we had no news. We were getting anxious. Bernard had mentioned stopping in Chile if they had problems, or Buenos Aires, Rio, or Saint Helena. In the letter he sent just before leaving, he said they might stop in Ascension Island since the normal route would take them close by. We were counting the miles, imagining the progress of the ketch. One month: They would be nearing Cape Horn. Two months: They would have arrived in Buenos Aires. Three months: We would get some news if they stopped in Ascension Island.

In early April, we received a fat envelope postmarked Alicante. On March 29, 1966, JOSHUA anchored in this Spanish harbor, more than four months after leaving Moorea. Bernard's letter related every detail of this non-stop passage, the longest ever made in a sailboat.

He described the storm they endured, "an end of the world gale." For six days, the boat was submitted to hurricane-strength winds which threw up enormous waves, "breakers 150 to 200 yards long, breaking without interruption for several hundred yards." Moitessier used all five of the lines they'd prepared in Tahiti, but JOSHUA still came within a hair of capsizing.

How had Vito Dumas managed? In 1942-43, the Argentinean sailor completed a solo circumnavigation by way of the three capes aboard LEGH II, a 31-foot double-ended ketch, without any of the mishaps that befell TZU HANG. Jean Merrien described Dumas' unique feat in his book, *Solo Sailors (Les Navigateurs Solitaires)*.

While Bernard watched the waves from under the dome, Françoise read him the passage where Dumas revealed his secret: In order to escape the fury of the sea, keep up your speed. Bernard immediately gave the helm to Françoise and leapt up on deck. There was no way he could bring back on board the lines with their 40-pound pig iron ballasts, nor the heavy net. He cut them with the Opinel knife he always kept razor sharp. Instantly JOSHUA was a different boat. Liberated, she became responsive once more, answering a deft touch on the helm to take the breaking waves on her quarter. For six days and six nights, Bernard for the first 26 hours, then Françoise as soon as the storm had somewhat abated, took turns at the inside helm. *"Françoise was turning into a helmswoman par excellence"*[2] said her husband, full of praise for his crew. *"We had total confidence in each other, we were in total agreement,"*[3] wrote Françoise.

On the night of January 10-11, after 49 days at sea, JOSHUA rounded Cape Horn, well offshore, in a moderate breeze. The only sign of land the crew saw was the blue smudge of the island of Diego Ramirez. The next day in the evening, a welcome and wonderful calm settled in. Bernard and Françoise could at last get some real sleep, and for the first time since Tahiti, they made love. Although they had to press hard to make it before the Easter holidays, the passage up the Atlantic was routine. Finally they made port in Spain and sent the long letter that reassured us.

Moitessier sent the story of his voyage to Jean Knocker, JOSHUA's designer. Their relationship was becoming closer. Knocker had become "his uncle by adoption," and Bernard's letters started with "Dear Uncle Jean." Knocker wrote to me:

April 10, 1966

Do you think we could suggest that he give a talk about his trip at Salle Pleyel [a Parisian conference hall]? That would be a way to get him some money and give us a chance to see him again. He's had a unique experience with that storm in the Pacific from which few people would have made it back. I suggested that he should hold out for a high fee. Maybe you could negotiate for him.

The magazine *Neptune nautisme* wanted to publish Moitessier's story. After being away for 18 months, Bernard was broke and couldn't be blamed if he hoped for a fee commensurate with his exploit.

Alicante, April 13, 1966

As far as money is concerned, this is a bit delicate since I shouldn't abandon *Bateaux* magazine. I have nothing against them, except that they offer less money than *Neptune*. Also, their format doesn't support the big spread with pictures and maps this article deserves. Still, it is not nice, so what the hell, at least it should be worth my while.

Moitessier was ambivalent toward money, due in part to the fact that he'd gone hungry for long periods during which he was happy if he could afford some *nuoc mam* for his rice. Now he was back, the kitty was empty. He needed money for himself, for Françoise and her children, and for the boat's upkeep. At the same time, he was aware that he had accomplished an extraordinary feat and that he should be paid accordingly for telling his story. He had respect for professionals like the book and magazine publishers who did a good job, but he was also weary of being exploited as a sea clown by people who were only interested in money.

He was offered a respectable fee and the story of his voyage was published in *Neptune nautisme* of June 1966 under the form of a "Letter to a Friend." It started like this: "We are now in Alicante, our first stop after 126 days at sea and 14,216 miles since Tahiti. No breakdowns, no mishaps. As we expected, we paid for it."

They were tired, the wind was blowing the wrong way. They decided to stop in Alicante. Françoise took the first train to Marseille to join the children for the Easter holidays. Bernard had kept his promise. She had not been separated for too long from the children. But the joy of being reunited with them was tempered by the difficulty of taking up life on land after such a long sea voyage. *"I was afraid; afraid of noise, people, cars, cities, the irrational fear of talking to a stranger, crossing a street . . . I wanted immediately to go back on the water."*[4]

In Alicante, Bernard set about writing his book. His letters came in quick succession.

April 24

Don't send us the TV people. It's quiet here. When the book comes out, we'll prostitute ourselves. It'll serve a purpose then.

May 26

I almost emptied an inkpot in a month. But it's not easy to avoid making the reader yawn. The passage was too long—no stopovers, no beachcombing.

It was nice of you to go to Editions Arthaud and inquire about their conditions and also to offer to introduce me there. But for now only one thing matters. I must finish my book properly, without screwing it up. It's hard work. No comparison with the first one, which just poured out of me.

May 31

I'll be in Paris shortly and it'll be a great pleasure to see you again. I'll bring you my 150 to 180 pages of scrawl. You'll give me your opinion as a pal, without worrying at this point if you are going to send it to Arthaud. It's much too early to think about the publisher.

By a lucky coincidence, the first book I published at Arthaud in the new series "Sea" was Miles Smeeton's book, *Once is Enough*. Bernard agreed to be published in the series. But he didn't get around to writing one sentence in August. Françoise and the children had joined him on JOSHUA for the summer. They were making their way back to France in short hops.

In September, the Moitessiers anchored JOSHUA in Bandol, where they rented an old house set among pine trees by the sea. Mamette, Bernard's mother, lived nearby. On land, he picked up his writing again with a vengeance. He had more room than on the boat, and a garden. He sent me the chapters as he wrote them and I returned them with my comments. Jacques Arthaud, too, passed along his ideas to Bernard who wrote to me expressing his concerns.

September 6, 1966

The passage from Tahiti to Alicante, as it stands, is long, boring, and unreadable. I made a big mistake in keeping a log and another in using it for the book in the last three months. I'm stuck, and I'm afraid I'll never untangle my-self unless someone else starts pruning. Would you do it?

The Salon Nautique (Paris Boat Show), scheduled for January, would be ideal for launching the book. The plan included bringing JOSHUA by truck to put her on display outside the exhibition hall. Bernard was intent on finishing the book on time.

November 5, 1966

If I hurry too much, the quality of the book will suffer. I must not do that. It was a special passage and it deserves a good book. But if it can be done, fine with me. As for bringing JOSHUA to Paris, it would be too much of an effort for me (taking out the masts, special trucking, etc.) and I would have a lot less energy for the book.

For obvious commercial reasons, Jacques Arthaud wanted the book to be ready for the Boat Show. He wrote to Bernard:

December 6, 1966

I would like your book to be launched at this time . . . We want as many people as possible to be aware of your amazing passage and it is therefore advisable to have as much publicity as possible. The Boat Show is the ideal venue. The award presentations and having your boat on show as well will give us the best media exposure. . . .

One month is far too short a time to publish a book, especially considering the holidays, but we will do our utmost to make it happen.

The author responded immediately:

December 8, 1966

I am ready to do everything possible, except spoil my book by rushing too much. On the other hand, I will not bring my boat to the show . . . I think it would be best for me to come to Paris to join the crew so we don't waste precious time corresponding by mail. But I have one condition: I must be satisfied with the text before I let you go to print. This book ought to be good and I'm determined not to botch it.

Bernard Moitessier and Jacques Arthaud were becoming friends. Jacques had been appointed director of the publishing house by his father, Benjamin Arthaud, who had founded Editions Arthaud in Grenoble. Jacques was keen on sports. He was a good skier and he owned a sailboat in which he cruised with his wife Anne-Marie and their three children, Florence, Jean-Marie, and Hubert. In 1964, when Eric Tabarly won the transatlantic race, Jacques hopped on the first plane and persuaded him to let Editions Arthaud publish his story. He himself wrote a book about a summer he spent among the Lapps and their reindeer.

Creativity and good business are sometimes at odds and

that can strain the relationship between publisher and author. But the relationship between Bernard and Jacques was very good, based on confidence and generosity. The Arthauds always had a warm welcome for Moitessier at their town house and Florence and Jean-Marie Arthaud's sailing careers were probably influenced by the time they spent in Bernard's company.

Cape Horn: the Logical Route was published January 7, 1967, with a print run of 20,000 copies, just in time for the Boat Show. I wrote a preface, recalling the author's earlier sailing experiences. Part of the work had already been published in *Neptune* magazine. In an appendix called Designer's Notes, Jean Knocker explained the choices that were made when JOSHUA was being built.

During the show, the French Sailing Union held its annual meeting. I had formed this association of cruisers four years earlier and in previous years our guests had been Commander Louis Lacroix, Eric Tabarly, and Jacques-Yves Le Toumelin. The new Cape-Horner agreed to make a presentation and tell the members about his formidable passage.

Until now, with his book *Sailing to the Reefs*, Moitessier seemed a likable but rather unlucky sailor. His adventures with Wakelam made them appear as comic book heroes, ingenious, funny, and not always ethical. All of a sudden, Bernard's character acquired a new dimension: He had become an outstanding sailor, who could be proud of himself. *"I had pulled off the biggest triumph of my life. Halfway around the world non-stop by way of Cape Horn . . . I didn't get puffed over it, nothing to worry about from that point of view. But you really won the lottery this time, old man, a stroke of luck for the ages."*[5]

During the Boat Show, the Moitessiers received the Golden Neptune. The Cruising Club of America presented Bernard with the prestigious Blue Water Medal, and the British awarded him the Wren Medal. The U.S. magazines published articles about his exploits. His "Letter to a Friend" was published in the German magazine, *Die Yacht.* He could be pleased with himself: *"You've got luck, baraka. Look closely: it's your escape velocity."*[6]

All kind of proposals followed, some crazy, some wonderful. François Spoerry, who built a new village in Port-Grimaud, offered Bernard a house and a slip if he would agree to leave on his next voyage from there. Looking back on 1967, Françoise had this to say: *"This was a happy year."*[7]

Did becoming a celebrity go to his head? Certainly not. Françoise noted: *"I am wondering if Bernard really liked being a celebrity or if he was simply flattered by the attention he received . . . He was becoming unstable, furious, impulsive and in fact was only dreaming of sailing again, leaving."*[8]

Suddenly the happiness disappeared. Moitessier tried to explain why in *Tamata and the Alliance.* The pressure from the publisher to finish *Cape Horn: the Logical Route* in time for the Boat Show caused him to make a slapdash job of the last three chapters. They consisted of the log he had written on board. *"I worked too quickly . . . No, not too quickly, not long enough . . . In those vital pages of the book, I had failed to transmit that sacred song from afar, that message from the skies. I had produced a fake."*[9]

September 1967. After the summer months and the sailing school, the succession of crews and cruises, and the thrill of sharing with his students the joy he derived from sailing and his love of the sea, fall found him discontented. *"I was left face to face with myself. I couldn't look myself in the mirror without wanting to spit in my face. On bookstore shelves, the book was like a finger pointing at my soul and saying: 'Traitor . . . you're a traitor . . . you've betrayed everything!'"*[10]

Bernard had lost what he called the "Alliance," being at peace with himself and with the universe. He was ashamed. He felt that by rushing the last chapters of the book, he'd failed to convey both the profound importance of his absorption into the great forces of nature and the incredible beauty of the high latitudes. *"I alone knew the crime I had committed. I couldn't confess it to anyone; even Françoise wouldn't have understood what I was talking about."*[11]

Apparently, he had entered a deep depression, and the book had served as a catalyst. In his search for perfection and truth, he felt he hadn't fulfilled the moral contract he'd made with himself. He had given me a hint of his trouble a year before.

November 30, 1966

I feel incredibly tired at the moment, I must say I am a
bit worried about my nerves.

For several months, he didn't write, as if he wanted to be alone with his fears, his moral exhaustion. He was extremely tired from all his years of frantic activity: building and fitting out JOSHUA, teaching one class after another at the sailing school, the route round Cape Horn, the storm, the four months at sea, and finally writing the book under so tight a deadline. It was possible, too, that his relationship with Françoise had changed. Maybe consciously or unconsciously the sailor regretted that he'd stopped roaming the sea to fulfill his promise to get her back quickly to the children, even though in doing so they'd accomplished such an outstanding passage.

He admitted, in *Tamata and the Alliance*, "October was devastating. Wrapped in total solitude, sucked down by a huge inner emptiness, I sank into the abyss." The Dragon was stirring. Moitessier was near madness. The ghost of his brother Françou haunted him, tempting him to suicide.

---

1. *Once is Enough.*
2. *Cape Horn: the logical route.*
3, 4, 7, 8. *60,000 Milles à la Voile.*
5, 6, 9, 10, 11. *Tamata and the Alliance.*

8

The great challenge

After each of his shipwrecks, which had left him naked, broke, and desperate, Bernard showed an extraordinary resilience, built himself a new boat, and resumed his voyages full of energy. But in the fall of 1967, he was in a deep depression and thought of suicide. Would he pull through?

Francis Chichester, a British sailor, winner of the first Solo TransAtlantic Race, had just accomplished an impressive feat. At the end of August 1966, aged 66, he left Plymouth alone on GIPSY MOTH IV, a 53-foot ketch, and reached Sydney on December 12, after sailing 14,000 miles in 107 days. He left Sydney on January 29 and arrived back in Plymouth, 15,517 miles and 119 days later. He had sailed around the world via the three capes making one stop only. He was knighted by Queen Elizabeth II.

The last great challenge that remained was to sail around the world solo and non-stop. Anyone attempting to do this would have to take on the harsh conditions of the Southern Ocean, risking breakdowns from leaks, torn sails, or even dismasting. They would be alone at sea for eight to 10 months, tired and uncomfortable, and with so little variety in their food that they might be inclined to skip meals. A mentally fragile sailor under such constant stress might reach the brink of madness.

Moitessier was feeling at an utter loss when a solution came to him, "like a bolt out of the blue." *"Since I had been a traitor by knocking off my book, what I had to do was to write another one to erase the first and lift the curse weighing on my soul."*[1] This new book would be written while at sea. It was the clearest, most luminous way to purge the remorse he felt. What the fortune-teller must have seen was the endless wake of a non-stop voyage around the world via the three capes. She had repeated, over and over: "I see water . . . water . . . lots and lots of water." Tahiti-Alicante had been merely a prologue, a dress rehearsal.

Bernard was suddenly revitalized. He spent the winter and spring preparing JOSHUA for the long journey. The four non-stop months from Polynesia to Spain had shown that with more and better equipment he could improve her performance. Bernard regretted not having had smaller, very sturdy sails that, even in strong winds, would have made the boat faster. Ferrari, the industrialist whom Baron Bich had encouraged to use Tergal, a polyester like Dacron, for the sails of his boat, gave him some of that material. Loiseau, the sailmakers, made several sails out of it, in all sizes, all well reinforced, and fitted the larger ones with several rows of reef points. Bernard fastened steps to the masts, to make it easier to climb them, and fitted a new bow pulpit. Stainless steel wire replaced the old galvanized standing rigging. Suddenly the faithful promoter of the block and tackle discovered the advantages of winches. Goïot gave him four sheet winches and two smaller winches to fit on the boom to make reefing easier. Previously, tightening the sheets with Attila had been difficult and consequently the jib was often not well trimmed. Also, because of the effort involved in reefing, he wouldn't take in a reef soon enough or he would delay shaking one out. Now, thanks to the winches and the new sails, JOSHUA's sails would be better set and she would tick off the miles more quickly without exhausting the skipper.

Getting ready included getting rid of excess weight. It's hard to imagine all the gear, some of it never used, that encumbers and slows down a long-distance sailboat.

"We had two old dinghies, one dead and the other ready to be thrown away, and at the same time an incredible amount of junk both small and large that I had accumulated over the years."[2] In Toulon, he threw off over 600 pounds of gear, including an old rotten jib, useless charts, and books.

I sent Bernard my best wishes for 1968. He wrote back:

January 8, 1968

I was very touched by your letter. I'll cherish it. I know it'll encourage me when times are difficult and I have to get my butt out of trouble by myself. It will remind me I have friends on land I want to see again and who would be happy to see me too.

All seemed to be in order—or almost. At the beginning of April, Bernard spent a week in Paris, and brought with him 30 pages. He had rewritten the last three chapters of *Cape Horn: the Logical Route* and asked Jacques Arthaud to substitute them in future print runs for the old ones that he was ashamed of. Before casting off for the Southern Ocean, he entrusted his publisher with what amounted to his will. He'd not forgotten he was leaving his wife Françoise behind. He discussed at length the terms of his contract. He wrote me about this in a letter dated March 10, 1968.

> My difficulties with Jacques arise mainly from the fact that this problem touches on the imponderable, while everything seems to imply that it's simply a matter of me bringing home the bacon. In reality, what I will need for this journey is something else, intangible and sacred . . .

An agreement was soon reached with Editions Arthaud. During the 10 months of Bernard's absence, Arthaud would pay a stipend to Françoise against the royalties for the book he would write after his circumnavigation.

During that busy week, Moitessier found the courage to visit the Ministry of Youth and Sport. He obtained a free haul out for JOSHUA at the Toulon navy yard, and free stores, gear, and cold weather clothing from the French Navy. The Beaulieu company loaned him a 16mm camera and he bought a large supply of color film. He spent part of the money he had available on a year's provisioning. Back from Paris, sipping a coffee in the harbor cafe while looking at JOSHUA's beautiful red hull across the road, the sailor was ready for a new adventure that would erase all his old debts. *"A feeling of total completeness filled my chest. It was one of those rare moments when life is racing full steam ahead while speaking very simply. All clear astern; all clear ahead."*[3]

At about the same time Bill King, a British sailor, was also getting ready for a non-stop circumnavigation. Other ambitious sailors had heard about the project. Trying to be the first to accomplish this feat, John Ridgway, who had rowed across the Atlantic with fellow paratrooper Chay Blyth, brought his departure forward by a year. Murray Sayle and Ron Hall, journalists with a British weekly, the *Sunday Times*, had a different concern: Bill King was sponsored by the *Sunday Express*, Ridgway by *People*, both papers competitors of the *Sunday Times*. How could they go one better? After mulling over the question, Sayle and Hall came up with an idea: their paper would organize a race for the first non-stop circumnavigation around these contenders.

To accommodate the independent spirit and feelings of the potential racers, they came up with a flexible organization. The competitors would have to leave from a British port between June 1 and October 31 and return to it after rounding the three capes. The requirements were few but harsh: no stops, no assistance, and no physical contact with anyone. Two prizes were offered: the Golden Globe, for the first one to reach his departure point after the circumnavigation, and a check for 5,000 pounds sterling for the fastest passage. The same contestant could win both prizes. The journalists hoped of course that Bernard Moitessier would participate. His Tahiti-Alicante passage made him the best candidate. Murray Sayle was dispatched to Toulon to entice the French sailor with a very attractive proposal.

"Are you Bernard?"

The sailor was enjoying his morning café-au-lait across from his boat when the man who'd addressed him explained that he was a journalist from a British weekly, the *Sunday Times*. The paper was organizing a solo non-stop sailing race around the world and was hoping that Moitessier would take part. Murray Sayle was convinced that Bernard would jump at the idea of winning the Golden Globe, or of collecting a check for 5,000 pounds.

Bernard was speechless, stunned. Finally he exploded: "This proposal makes me want to throw up." He was indignant. With a few words, his visitor had destroyed the serenity and the certitude he had regained at such cost. It was close to sacrilege to turn his ultimate challenge into a race. The Southern Ocean, its exacting, awe-inspiring beauty, and the three capes that mark its boundaries, were not a vacant lot on which to hold a circus. He expressed his anger in an article in *Bateaux*, a sailing magazine. "In a passage like this, a man must look into himself without facing a competitor. I disapprove of a race; it makes you lose sight of the essential: a voyage to your own utter limits, this search for a profound truth with as sole witnesses the sea, the wind, the boat, the infinitely big, the infinitely small."

Besides the fact that it would be an outrage to turn this adventure into a contest, there was also a huge technical difference. A long-distance voyage made at the sailor's own rhythm was very different from a race in which the need to be the fastest means taking on extra risks.

Moitessier turned his back on the thunderstruck journalist. A week later, Murray Sayle tried again, politely and persistently emphasizing the flexibility of the rules that left Moitessier free to start when and where he wanted. In England, everyone was talking about the race. Ten boats were getting ready to take the start.

Bernard had thought about nothing else since their meeting the week before. To Sayles's utter amazement, he announced: "I'll be leaving Toulon as soon as possible for Plymouth, where I will start the race."

When asked why he changed his mind, Moitessier explained: "Not many of us will make it to the finish line. Perhaps none. But suppose the gods grant that I return safely and that I'm also both the first one home and the fastest. In that case, I'll snatch the check without saying thank you, coolly auction off the Golden Globe, and leave without a word for the *Sunday Times*. That way, I'll make a public statement of the contempt I feel for your paper's project."

There was also a practical reason. Facing the Gulf of

Lion, the Bay of Biscay, and the English Channel while sailing from Toulon to Plymouth would amount to a rigorous sea trial. A sailor and his boat are never quite ready, especially for such an extended voyage. Coping with the Atlantic Ocean swells and the difficult approach to the English Channel would give Moitessier an opportunity to refine the last details.

Besides, the 5,000-pound prize was nothing to sneeze at. He had spent most of his publisher's advance on fitting out JOSHUA. This again was typical of his attitude toward money. He needed it but was not very proud of what he had to do in order to get it. As a result, he despised the people who forced him to ask. Nevertheless he developed a pleasant rapport with Murray Sayle. Both men had stated their position and each understood and respected where the other was coming from. They continued their conversation over dinner in a restaurant in the harbor and over coffee in JOSHUA's cabin. Moitessier said firmly: "I've decided to leave from England because it suits me from every point of view. Each of us will run the race he wants to. I'll run my race, on my terms."

Suddenly he became impatient. He wrote to me:

I have a lot of work. JOSHUA has become a very beautiful sailboat, much better than before. I'm itching to go sailing. JOSHUA is being hauled out on May 13 and should be ready on May 27. I'm tempted to take off as quickly as possible for a test sail to England, where I'll find a friendly nautical milieu, the gear I need, and I'll be able to see what's what.

Bernard turned down, as attractive as it was, François Spoerry's offer of a house in a new development in Port-Grimaud. He clung to his freedom.

When he left Toulon for Plymouth, Françoise and Michel, a reliable crewmember, went with him. Françoise took a hundred reels of Bernard at work on the deck. She used them for the films she made later: *Bateau et Capitaine, La Mer,* and *Oceans.*

In Plymouth JOSHUA tied up alongside CAPTAIN BROWNE. Bernard's old friend, Loïck Fougeron, who had sailed with him from Casablanca to the Canary Islands, was also entering the Golden Globe race. CAPTAIN BROWNE was a 30-foot steel cutter, designed by Louis Van de Wiele. After sailing around the world, Louis and Annie Van de Wiele had had it built for a yearlong cruise to the West Indies. Fougeron bought it from them.

Millbay Dock was virtually derelict. The décor was not very alluring—freighters that used it came mainly to load scrap iron—but it was quiet, and the dockside berthing within easy reach of boatyards and chandleries made it an ideal place to prepare for long distance voyaging. Nigel Tetley was also there, fitting out VICTRESS. Tetley, 44, a lieutenant commander in the Royal Navy, was living with his wife aboard the 40-foot-long, 22-foot-wide, plywood ketch-rigged trimaran. He had been a few months away from retirement when the race was announced and he decided to enter. Nigel and Bernard became fast friends, helping each other and often eating together. Bill King, the first to enter the race, was also preparing his boat in Plymouth, but their contact with him was less frequent.

Bernard didn't meet the other entrants: the British sailors John Ridgway and Chay Blyth (who had rowed across the Atlantic together) both on 30-foot fiberglass monohulls; Donald Crowhurst, a 36-year-old electronics engineer, on a 40-foot trimaran; Robin Knox-Johnston, a merchant marine captain; and a last minute candidate, Alex Carrozzo, an Italian sailor, on a 66-foot cold-molded wooden ketch.

Knox-Johnston, 29 at the time, was in good physical and mental shape. Unable to find financing to build the yacht of his dreams, he fitted out his 32-foot ketch, SUHAILI. Imbued with British pride, he couldn't accept that any but a British sailor should win this race. He knew his boat was slower than JOSHUA and, as a result, decided to leave as quickly as possible.

Knox-Johnston left Falmouth on June 14. John Ridgway had left even earlier, on June 2. But by the time Moitessier reached England, the paratrooper had already abandoned the race on July 16 and headed for Recife in Brazil to repair the deck of his boat, which wasn't up to this kind of extreme sailing and started to lift. Chay Blyth left on June 8. He disqualified himself on August 15 in Tristan da Cunha where he requested fuel from GILLIAN GAGGINS, a cargo ship from South Africa that three times a year took supplies to the island. He tied DYSTICUS III, his fiberglass 30-footer, off the ship's stern and went on board for a hot shower and a drink. The mechanics from the ship fixed his electrical generator. No outside assistance was permitted for the race. Blyth continued outside of the race but gave up after his wind vane broke.

While the first competitors were already at sea, with varying success, Bernard and Loïck were hard at work. Dany and I were on our way back from a cruise in Norway on our boat and put in to Plymouth to say good-bye. Bernard came for dinner on our ketch CORSEN. He noticed the jacklines running from stem to stern on each side of the deck providing a place to clip the tether of a safety harness in heavy weather. He had already discussed this arrangement with Bill King and immediately installed it on his own boat.

Both French skippers had endless job lists and fitting out the boats was a balancing act. They didn't want to forget anything that they would need but neither did they want to overload their boats. Bernard knew from experience that the key to speed and safety was a light boat. He was on the lookout for the unessential. He got rid of a ton of gear: anchor windlass, engine, four anchors, 900 pounds of chain, dinghy, books, charts, *Sailing Directions* that didn't cover the present route, spare zinc anodes, paint, ropes. He put it all in storage so he could retrieve it when he came back. Nicole Van de Kerchove, a French sailor, came to help her friend Loïck Fougeron. Françoise helped with the final preparations and with stowing the fresh provisions. She drove back and forth nine times between Bandol and Plymouth, but she was already beginning to feel that she was simply being useful: *"He didn't see me, his mind was already on the open sea."* [4]

The *Sunday Times* journalists gave each sailor a watertight camera with remote shutter release and lots of film, and the paper's photographer gave them advice. They even tried to convince Bernard to take along a radio transmitter so he could send them news twice a week. But Bernard refused to take aboard such a heavy, awkward, and somewhat burdensome contraption. Besides, in a boat lit by kerosene lamps, the energy needed for feeding the transmitter wasn't available. For sending a message, he said, laughing, nothing could beat a slingshot. It was light, precise, efficient. He bought a small recorder so he could record weather forecasts captured by his receiver.

Everything was ready, except for the weather, which delivered a miserable diet of rain and westerly winds. In the meantime, Bernard found time to answer my letter sending him my good wishes:

Plymouth, August 20

Thank you for your wise and friendly letter. It's nice of you to think of us from time to time, but don't remember just the French sailors, we are all *in the same boat!*

Loïck and I have been waiting for the last few days for a 36-hour more-or-less-favorable weather window to get away from the Channel and give the Bay of Biscay a wide berth.

Two days later, on Thursday, August 22, the weather forecast promised a northeast wind. JOSHUA had to set sail at once. Waiting until the next day was out of the question—all sailors know it's unlucky to leave on a Friday. Françoise sobbed while

Bernard tried to console her: *"Listen, we'll be seeing each other again soon! After all, what are eight or nine months in a lifetime?"*[5]

She had guessed that his self-centeredness was Moitessier's driving force. He admitted it in *The Long Way*: *"I felt such a need to rediscover the wind of the high sea, nothing else counted at that moment, neither earth nor men. All JOSHUA and I wanted was to be left alone with ourselves. Any other thing did not exist, had never existed."*[6]

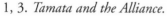

1, 3. *Tamata and the Alliance.*
2, 5, 6. *The Long Way.*
4. *60,000 Milles à la Voile.*

9

In harmony with
the universe

Under full sail and pushed at seven knots by a nice northeast breeze, JOSHUA took the start on Thursday, August 22, 1968, CAPTAIN BROWNE in her wake. Françoise, aboard a launch, fought back her tears and shouted: *"You can't imagine how lovely she looks."*[1] The ketch rounded Plymouth's outer breakwater; her red hull faded into the fog. The launch turned around. Back on land, Françoise and Nicole de Kerchove shared their sadness. Nicole said:

"We have to get organized waiting for them."

Françoise, lucid, replied, "You're dreaming. They will never return to Plymouth."

On the open sea Moitessier was alone, and happy.

He was also very tired. While getting ready he'd been constantly under stress and had lost seven pounds. Because of the fog, he had to keep watch on deck for the first 24 hours.

By the time the two French sailors left, SUHAILI had almost reached the latitude of the Cape of Good Hope. Robin Knox-Johnston knew that his 32-foot ketch was slower than Moitessier's boat. For the first 16 days, he made only 75 miles per day. JOSHUA was going twice as fast. In four days, Bernard crossed the Channel and the Bay of Biscay and reached the latitude of Vigo, with one 178-mile day. Was he being competitive? In his first meeting with Murray Sayle, he had expressed a strong disapproval of the race.

He worried about Loïck and Bill King because he knew that in poor visibility the risk of collision in the heavily traveled shipping lanes was high. Listening to the BBC, he was disappointed to hear no mention of the race. Since his only means of communication was his slingshot, he had to rely on chance encounters with other ships to let family and friends know that all was well on board. He'd painted the name of the boat in big black letters on the white of the cockpit coaming so that freighters wouldn't need to approach too closely to read it. JOSHUA carried aloft the code-flag signal MIK, which means, "Transmit my position to Lloyds."

He drove JOSHUA at full speed, setting too much canvas and even going so far as to rig a storm jib as a studding sail out of the sheer joy of being at sea again. Reducing the weight in the boat had transformed her, and made a great difference to her performance. The weight distribution was much improved, too, with most of it concentrated in the center and the forward and aft compartments almost empty.

In October, sailing in a southwesterly gale, Bernard was thrilled with how the heavy steel hull behaved. *"The sea is often heavy and JOSHUA surfs at times. The bow lifts much better than before."*[2] Although Bernard had left ashore a ton of gear in Plymouth, JOSHUA had still gained back 1,200 pounds, even with only 100 gallons of fresh water aboard, half a ton less than when he'd left Tahiti. But that wasn't enough. Nearing the Forties, Moitessier threw overboard what he considered expendable: a box of army biscuits, a case of condensed milk, 25 bottles of wine, rice, sugar, and a case of preserves. The hungry vagabond of MARIE-THÉRÈSE II would have given anything for such bounty. But this time, the stakes were different. Keeping track of his consumption, he figured he had sufficient stores for eight months at sea.

Before reaching the high southern latitudes, in anticipation of heavy weather, he changed the mizzen and the mainsail for strongly reinforced smaller sails without battens and with three rows of reef points. To concentrate the weight amidships, he stowed the fair-weather sails on the cabin sole. Even under reduced sail, in a fresh breeze, JOSHUA reached good speeds for a vessel of her type.

If Bernard was thinking of winning the Golden Globe and taking the 5,000-pound check without a thank you to the *Sunday Times*, as he had stated, he didn't allude to it at this stage of his story in *The Long Way*.

On September 29, he was in sight of the island of Trindade, off the coast of Brazil. He hoped to be spotted so his passage would be signaled and his loved ones reassured. *"If the* Sunday Times *got a radio message from Trindade, the BBC might announce that* JOSHUA *had been sighted on such and such day, and give positions for Bill King and Nigel as well.* "[3] Bernard was glued to the British radio, but he heard no mention of his competitors' positions. In fact Tetley had just left England on September 16.

While Moitessier was at 20° S, Fougeron, going much more slowly, was only at the latitude of the Cape Verde Islands. Bill King had left two days after CAPTAIN BROWNE and was only 500 miles ahead. Despite his boat being 12 feet longer, he was making only about 110 miles a day under his junk rig, which wasn't proving very effective. Knox-Johnston had rounded the Cape of Good Hope on September 13, and had already covered one third of the Indian Ocean.

Moitessier knew none of this; he received no information on his fellow travelers throughout the voyage. He thought of them and of his friends on land: *"You are alone, yet not alone; the others need you and you need them. Without them you would not get anywhere and nothing would be true."*[4]

JOSHUA entered the strong westerlies and charged toward the Cape of Good Hope with one day's run of 182 miles in a week in which he covered 1,112 miles. On October 20, near the Cape of Storms, he sailed toward Walker Bay. It was a Sunday and he was hoping to meet a yacht: *"I would surely get news of Loïck, Bill King, and Nigel."*[5] But the wind was blowing Force 7 and no yachts were out. Bernard had to attract the attention of a small Greek freighter. With his slingshot, he hurled onto its foredeck a weighted aluminum can in which he had stuffed a message asking the freighter to slow down. The watch officer aboard ORIENT TRANSPORTER saw the projectile land on the deck and twirled a forefinger at his temple, as if he thought Bernard was mad. Bernard finally made himself understood. He managed to throw onto the deck a package containing a copy of his log and film he had exposed since his departure. He asked for it to be sent to family and friends so they would have news of him. A few days later, the *Sunday Times* printed a picture of JOSHUA under full sail. But it came at a high price. While the cargo ship was maneuvering to leave, her overhanging stern struck the ketch. The mainmast was lucky to survive and the bowsprit was twisted 45° to port. Bernard had to use a block and tackle to straighten it.

———— ∞ ————

At that point SUHAILI was one ocean ahead of JOSHUA: She was south of Cape Leeuwin and just completing her Indian Ocean passage. Tetley's trimaran was a disappointment. It was supposed to be very fast but had only averaged 64 miles a day during the first week. Based on the performance of the competitors thus far, the *Sunday Times* estimated the amount of time they would take and when they were likely to reach England. Knox-Johnston would take 330 days and be back in Falmouth on May 10. Bill King would take 270 days, Tetley 319, and Fougeron 339. Moitessier would buckle it up in only 246 days, arriving in Plymouth on April 24, and would be the first one home. By far the fastest, he would take the big prize.

He knew nothing of all this and could not care less.

The Southern Hemisphere spring and summer of 1968-1969 were much milder than expected, given the bad reputation the high latitudes had. Moitessier hadn't forgotten the hurricane that had threatened his boat during the passage from Tahiti to Alicante. His first taste of what the region could deliver was a gale on October 12, which he weathered with two reefs in the mizzen and a 38-square-foot storm jib. It was very short-lived and gave JOSHUA, under this shortened sail, two days of 182 and 173 miles.

Shortly after rounding the Cape of Good Hope, in a moderate gale, the ketch encountered confused breaking seas. Twice JOSHUA was knocked flat by combers, her masts almost horizontal, but she suffered no damage. At parallel 39, she encountered strong easterly winds, and stuck to her course under double-reefed sails. The good weather then returned and stayed until they reached the Pacific Ocean. *"I think we are having an unusual year,"* thought Moitessier. *"I haven't felt the need to clip myself on since Good Hope . . . and I have a beautiful tan just as if in the trade winds."*[6] These conditions lasted two months. At 42°S, the temperature in the cockpit was 75°F at noon. At 40°S, Moitessier went on deck naked to take a sight.

***

On December 17, JOSHUA was nearing the south coast of Tasmania. Peter Nichols in his book about the race, *Voyage for Madmen,* wrote: "Varley Wisby and his two sons, fishing off the southwest coast of Tasmania, saw a red-hulled ketch coming straight for them. On deck a lone man was flashing a small mirror, catching the sunlight." The fishermen described the sailor as "emaciated beneath a filthy wool sweater and baggy black pants, his hair and gray-streaked beard as long and wild as a yogi's." A skillful maneuver brought the fishing boat close alongside JOSHUA. Bernard threw them a tin can, asking them to give it to the commodore of the yacht club, and chatted with the three men for a little while. *"No one could give me news of my friends. Someone had heard something about an English yachtsman who rounded New Zealand without having stopped."*[7] This had to have been Knox-Johnston who by then was half way between New Zealand and Cape Horn. Nigel Tetley was in the middle of the Indian Ocean, near Amsterdam Island. Fougeron and Bill King had both given up. On October 31, in a big storm in the South Atlantic both their sailboats had been capsized and had sustained serious damage. Fougeron turned back toward Saint Helena. GALWAY BLAZER, dismasted, headed for Cape Town.

Also on October 31, the last day to enter the race, Donald Crowhurst, a British sailor, left on TEIGNMOUTH ELECTRON, a 40-foot trimaran. Alex Carrozzo left, too, but would abandon the race a few days later suffering from an ulcer.

Only four competitors remained in the race around the world: Knox-Johnston, Moitessier, Tetley, and Crowhurst.

1, 2, 3, 4, 5, 6, 7. *The Long Way.*

10

What race?

While Moitessier had no news of the other competitors, this was not the case for those of them who had two-way radios. For Robin Knox-Johnston, the race had almost ended in New Zealand. On November 11, he entered Otago Bay after 159 days at sea. He had arranged to meet Bruce Maxwell, a *Sunday Times* journalist. SUHAILI, becalmed and unable to maneuver, ran aground: *"I lashed the warp to the anchor, stripped off and jumped in. For the first 10 yards, I walked along the bottom into deeper water, carrying the anchor . . . When the water rose above my mouth, I began bouncing up for air every few paces. Eventually I dived down and dug the fluke into the sand."*[1] Two fishermen offered a hand but he turned them down because accepting help would have disqualified him from the race.

At high tide, the ketch floated free and her skipper moved her into deeper water. Bruce Maxwell gave Robin news of his family but the rules forbade the receiving of mail, which would be considered outside assistance. Knox-Johnston learned from Maxwell that Moitessier was 4,000 miles behind. "Bruce said that if I kept going at the same rate as I had made to date, a neck and neck finish between Moitessier and myself was being predicted."

The British sailor's motives were easy to understand: he wanted to win and was excited at the idea of competing with his main adversary. Moitessier's attitude was more complex, even ambiguous. Winning the Golden Globe would signify a magnificent recovery from the two MARIE-THÉRÈSE shipwrecks. It would prove what a formidable sailor he had become and would be a tribute to his boat, to the strength of its construction, and to the architect who created it. And he would collect the money, with no apologies.

At the same time, his journey was taking on another dimension. Facing a long period of calms off the coast of Australia, he was not worrying about the race. Normally, competitors in a race or a regatta try to avoid windless areas, knowing that if they get stuck in a high-pressure area, a smarter or luckier racer will steal the honors. For Moitessier, the calms were a gift from God.

After rounding the Cape of Good Hope, he'd experienced a period of extreme fatigue. He blamed this setback on the collision with the cargo ship. His back hurt and his muscles were weak. Already underweight when he left Plymouth, he'd lost another two pounds. On top of that, the stomach ulcer he suffered from periodically had resurfaced. He was in a general state of exhaustion, he was becoming clumsy, and his movements and reflexes were slow. "In my present weakened state, I'm asking JOSHUA to do her best." He was near the longitude of Mauritius, and Bernard couldn't help looking at the chart or at the small globe DAMIEN's crew had given him when they were preparing for their own circumnavigation. Mauritius was only two weeks away. It would be warm there under the trade winds. He could pick up where he'd left off with his generous friends and rediscover the happiness he'd known there.

But he pressed on. And these days of calms on a smooth sea brought him the rest he needed: hours of sleep without worry. He began to eat better and regained his strength. As Doctor Stern-Veyrin and the other doctors he had seen before leaving had told him, it was the stress on land, the constant running around, that caused his ulcer. Here, he had regained his inner peace.

The race? What race?

⊶∽⊷

This long period of good weather, unusual for the Southern Ocean, didn't mean that life aboard JOSHUA was now free of weariness and danger.

In the second half of the Pacific Ocean, Moitessier encountered a gale. In white seas, the boat tore along under single-reefed staysail, storm jib, and mainsail, with the mizzen furled. Aboard a lighter, better rigged, better prepared JOSHUA, Moitessier was euphoric. "I have been at the foot of the mast for hours now, ready to drop the main." But he couldn't bring himself to do it. "JOSHUA is tearing along on the very edge between too much and not enough, on immense seas carpeted with long, pale sheets of foam." At night, the ketch carried the storm jib, the staysail single-reefed, and the mainsail double-reefed. The wind increased to Force 9. *"I ought to drop the main entirely, and perhaps the staysail. JOSHUA would still do very well and stay this side of going too fast. But we're surfing; it's breath-taking at times."*[2]

Over a period of six hours, JOSHUA averaged eight knots, at times reaching 10 knots. In the bioluminescent sea, JOSHUA was like a flame running in the night. On one surfing run of more than 20 yards, a great plume of spray burst upwards from both sides of the bow. *"The entire sea is white and the sky as well. I no longer quite know where I am, except that we long ago crossed the boundary of too much. But never have I felt my boat like that; never has she given me that much."*[3]

Madly happy, ecstatic even, he began to think, "Why not keep going, indefinitely?"

On February 3, 1969 JOSHUA was less than 300 miles from Cape Horn. Bernard took advantage of a clearing to take a perfect sight by removing the scope from the sextant and using both eyes to ensure he had the sun on the horizon and not on the back of a wave. The ketch was 218 miles from Cape Horn's outpost, the island of Diego Ramirez. Bernard spent the night on deck, very tired, but also excited. The next day, at noon, the sky cleared, and the sun shining in the blue sky created a fantastic light. While the wind still blew at Force 7 to 9 from the north-northwest, the sea became a deep blue and subsided. By parallel 56, the cabin temperature was 57°F. They rounded Diego Ramirez about five miles off. The wind freshened to Force 9, and the boat ran under reefed staysail and storm jib. Moitessier admitted: "I'm worn out." On a very clear night, the wind eased to Force 5 or 6 and Cape Horn appeared, pale under the moon. Stars glittered, and in the south, Antarctica gave off its white loom. Moitessier hove-to, so as to see the Horn in daylight. Then, exhausted, he let the boat sail eastward. He prepared a good dinner of canned lobster and crayfish and washed it down with his third bottle of champagne (one for each cape) while the ketch made her way, at last, into the Atlantic Ocean.

JOSHUA was south of Cape Horn on February 5. SUHAILI had been there just two weeks before. Neither Bernard nor Robin knew where the other was. Knox-Johnston's radio wasn't transmitting and the organizers of the Golden Globe had had no news of him for four and a half months, since he left New Zealand behind. They were concerned about him until, on April 6, a cargo ship sighted him near the Azores.

After his encounter with the fishermen in Tasmania, Moitessier fashioned some model boats, to which he attached canisters containing messages, and threw them into the ocean off New Zealand. Nobody saw him at Cape Horn. He tried to make himself seen near the Falklands. *I wanted people to know I wasn't dead.*[4] Hoping he'd meet a fisherman or the port pilot, he wrote a letter to Jacques Arthaud. But tacking into the strong contrary wind up the sound toward Port Stanley at night would have been dangerous. He beat to within half a mile of the lighthouse and signaled with his mirror. He got no response and left not knowing if he'd been seen. But he had been, and his passage was signaled to the *Sunday Times* which confirmed that he would probably finish the winner, around April 25.

He surmised that Bill King, with his fast boat, was nearing Plymouth. He was extremely exhausted from the stress of rounding Cape Horn and pushing JOSHUA to her limit. He put JOSHUA on a northeasterly course, pointing her toward the region where the chart showed no more icebergs, and, perhaps, beyond that, toward the trade winds. Bernard adopted what he called a "heaving-to of the mind," a kind of intellectual hibernation, while he regained his strength.

The journalists of the British weekly, as landlubbers will, began readying a welcome for the winner. Did they have any idea what was going through the minds of the sailors? They had now been facing extreme conditions for a long period of time, utterly alone. How did they manage everyday life? Were they at the end of their tethers, both physically and mentally? Did they have enough stores and fresh water? How did their gear hold out? How did they cope with the inevitable damage to their boats? The transmissions from Knox-Johnston, which had ceased several months before, and the logbook pages Moitessier had sent from the Cape of Good Hope and Tasmania provided only partial answers.

The reality would only be known by reading between the lines in the narratives written much later by the two principal heroes of the Golden Globe. Knox-Johnston, a professional mariner, wrote about his joy at being at sea even though his boat was slow, it leaked, and the self-steering gear broke. *"I don't know with whom I would like to change places."*[5] Such was not the case for Ridgway, the paratrooper, who, breaking down in tears after a difficult time reducing sail, realized he was crying every day and gave up. It was too much for him.

Bernard Moitessier had been very happy since the start. *"I couldn't ask for more; I have it all."*[6] He was in total harmony with his sailboat, with the wind, and with the universe. He enjoyed the endless riches of the sea. He watched with affection all the teeming life of the ocean: the albatross, malamocks, Cape pigeons, the fishes swimming alongside. He took pictures, filming moments of this life so others could share their magic. In calm weather, he fed the sea birds, and tamed them to the point where one of them took a piece of cheese from his fingers. Dolphins accompanied him, guided him, and when they warned him of a rock toward which he was heading, were happy that he had understood their message. Time meant nothing. Days followed nights amid the beautiful colors of the sea and the sky, under the splendor of the aurora australis.

Like his hero Joshua Slocum, and many solo sailors, Bernard talked to himself, giving himself orders or commenting on his actions. So as to be in intimate contact with nature and the elements, and to be more in harmony with the movements of the sailboat, except in very heavy weather he went barefoot. *"There is not much to do on a boat. But there is much to feel."*[7]

He followed a routine that suited him. In the morning, he heated up a cup of coffee, rolled his first cigarette, and ate a large bowl of oatmeal. At 10 a.m., he snacked on pâté and army biscuits. Then it was lunch, a nap, and tea at 4 p.m. At nightfall he took a short nap, then got up and spent some time in the cockpit. He rolled himself another cigarette, made a hot cup of Ovaltine, a cup of coffee and then slept again. Sometimes he had to stand watch. In heavy weather, the fatigue would come back and he would heave to. But when the good weather returned, he could sleep all day. *"I am happy. It is wonderful to be that free."*[8] Weather permitting, he would perch on the pulpit for the sheer pleasure of watching the bow slice its way through the ocean. He spent the days maintaining the rigging to prevent the sails, the halyards, and the sheets from chafing. He oiled the log, adjusted the self-steering mechanism. This was his routine.

The dorados and tuna caught with the trolling line improved his daily fare. An uninspired cook, he took little pleasure in preparing his meals. The fresh food he took on in Plymouth, like the roast Françoise had cooked, was but a memory. His diet consisted of rice, pasta, dehydrated vegetables, sea biscuits spread with butter or jam, and the ever-present and nourishing Ovaltine, as in the days of Indochina and MARIE-THÉRÈSE. Grapefruit, lemons, and onions kept for a long time. Bernard drank little wine: about 15 bottles over seven months. One evening he tried a strange confection of lettuce hearts, lard, onions, tomato puree, and sugar lumps, to which he added half a pound of camembert cut in little cubes. He let it simmer for a long time and was astonished that the result did not live up to his efforts.

Provisioning was the only area in which he'd failed to prepare adequately. He hadn't put on board some samples of canned food that a manufacturer had sent him. Had he known how delicious they were, he would have bought several cases. In heavy weather he had no appetite, cooking was difficult, and he ate poorly, aggravating his fatigue. It was a vicious circle.

At Christmas time, he missed his family and friends. To cheer himself up, he unwrapped a big, perfectly preserved smoked ham and opened one of the bottles of champagne Jean Knocker had given him to celebrate the rounding of each of the three capes.

He read every day, avidly. He read and reread the same six or seven books: The *Roots of Heaven, Zorba, The Jungle Book*, a treatise on yoga left on board by a crewmember.

His happiness at being at sea was not unalloyed. His frame of mind fluctuated with the weather. In the doldrums, with its calms and rain, he lost his appetite and his vigor. After the Cape of Good Hope, he was completely exhausted. But after discovering yoga, he found an inner peace, a deep serenity. "We are alone, my boat and I. Alone with the immensity of the sea for us alone." Sailing was the road to find inner peace, *"the search for a truth I had lost perhaps but which was slowly coming back to life in the boat's wake."*[9]

He wrote in his log that all debts would be paid. But what debts? Losing his boats? Most likely. The questionable ethics he adopted in Durban, Cape Town, and France, in order not to starve? There were other scars, perhaps more intimate. In the Indian Ocean, Bernard was able to hear Radio Saigon. He made a cruel discovery: *"After twenty years away from my native land, I hardly understand the language I used to speak fluently."*[10]

This was worse than nostalgia, it was like a betrayal of Asia and *"the richest, most formative period of my life."*[11]

Whatever haunted Bernard probably had older, deeper roots: the breaking off with his childhood friends, the pals in Rach Gia who had become his enemies and at whom in a fratricidal war he had aimed his rifle, the tragedy that brought Françou to commit suicide. Perhaps, to subdue the Dragon and pay off all the debts, he had to trail this wake forever.

———— ∞∞ ————

1, 5. *A World of My Own.*
2, 3, 4, 6, 7, 8, 9, 10, 11. *The Long Way.*

11

—◦◦◦◦◦—

Going home does not make sense

Four months passed, five months. But could this voyage be measured in terms of days and weeks? *"JOSHUA has taken me beyond my dreams, where time has ceased to exist."*[1] The lone sailor had achieved total freedom. He was in perfect harmony with the sea, the sky, and the wind. He was in no hurry to get back. What did he want? "To live only with the sea and my boat, for the sea and my boat. To forget the land, its pitiless cities, its blind crowds, and its senseless activities." Studying the globe, he slowly came to this truth: *"Leaving from Plymouth and returning to Plymouth now seems like leaving from nowhere to go nowhere."*[2] But what about the race? Why not return to Europe, pick up the 5,000 pounds, and take off again without stopping, in a huge affront to the *Sunday Times* and its offensive scheme?

He thought money was evil. Europe was not his mother-land. His true country was Asia where he'd lived until he was 26 and known his richest years. Enchanted by the sea, he was tempted to go on indefinitely. *"JOSHUA will continue its wake in the ocean for the sheer joy of creating foam spray."*[3] The ketch was up to the task. The gear had held up perfectly. The lockers still had four months of supplies, the tanks 40 gallons of freshwater that he could replenish with rain. He might run out of to-bacco. But what about the man himself? Fatigued, he might overestimate his strength and his endurance. Fall had arrived in the Southern Hemisphere, with its strong winds, its cold, its more dangerous seas, and its shorter days.

Then again, where would he go? He thought of Mauritius. But it did not offer the peace and quiet he would need to write his book. He remembered how he'd communed with nature and the universe in the Galápagos. He would find the silence and solitude he needed to be creative. The archipelago was suf-ficiently remote and hard to reach that journalists wouldn't come to pester him. He planned to drop his anchor there. This meant he would have to once more endure the Indian Ocean and a large part of the Pacific with their storms before reaching the trade winds, then sail another 4,000 miles to the enchanted archipelago. Or should he stop in Tahiti? Either way, it was going to be very tough going and very long. To go on sailing after more than six months at sea, wasn't this pure madness?

When he first thought about it, a moment of reason told him not to make an immediate decision. He would make up his mind after rounding the Horn.

Robin Knox-Johnston was similarly tempted: *"My first*

impulse on rounding the Horn was to keep on going east. This im-
pulse was a way of cocking a snook at the Southern Ocean itself.
A spell of cold uncomfortable weather quickly put things back into
their proper perspective. I thought of hot baths, pints of beer, the
other sex, and steaks, and turned up into the Atlantic for home." [4]

Bernard started worrying about the risks involved in sending a package to a ship in the vicinity of the Cape of Good
Hope, where gale follows gale. He was still affected by the collision JOSHUA had suffered, and which could have sunk her, the
last time he was there. He vacillated, changing his mind almost
with the winds. As it turned out, the conditions were fine and
the sea offered him rare pleasures.

In his log, on February 21, he was ecstatic: "I almost see
Venus setting, so clear is the sky."

The difficult passage of the "hard cape" as the earlier sailors
referred to Cape Horn, beating to windward off the Falklands,
the disappointment of not delivering a message, and the hazards
of making a contact off the Cape of Good Hope, all convinced
him not to continue eastward. On February 28, he wrote in his
log: "I am giving up. My instinct tells me it is best."

A moderate gale three days earlier had left him exhausted.
He was afraid of going too far, of not being able to hold out for
another four months, three of them in the high latitudes, to
round the Cape of Good Hope, Tasmania, and New Zealand.
To his way of thinking, to give up was to steer north, toward
the warmth of the trade winds and the sun and regain there
some of the strength he'd lost. Returning to Europe would let
him reassure his friends by signaling his passage at Saint Helena
or Ascension Island. He would see his family again, and his

mother. He would also retrieve the gear he'd taken off JOSHUA and left in Plymouth and that he could use. Finally, he might "as well just put in a little effort, try to pick up the *Sunday Times* prize." This was what he called "giving up."

On March 11, he confided in the small recorder he had taken along: "The sun is shining, the sea is virtually flat, wind force 0 to 1, the sails hardly move. JOSHUA's speed is a quarter of a knot . . . At times like this, all the debts are paid up."

With the good weather he was regaining his strength. A few days of calm seas and light breezes were enough. The truth prevailed. The mere idea of returning to Europe made him sick, as if his senses had *"picked up the fetid smell of the Dragon. The stink came from the north, in gusts."*[5] He would keep going, because he was happy at sea and for another unexplainable reason. Several times he'd had the feeling that he had approached the fourth dimension but without being able to touch it. In his search for the absolute, he was getting close to some sort of mystical revelation: *"The sea is telling me things I am beginning to understand. I want to go further. I feel there is something. I have to go, I cannot think about how to get back."* He also said: *"I am at peace with the whole universe. I found happiness in this small world I created."*[6]

Near the Cape of Good Hope, the commercial traffic was dense. Moitessier passed close to a large Russian trawler, and showed his MIK flags hoping that the ship would signal having seen JOSHUA. In that area the sea was alive with birds and seals that swam fearlessly up to the boats. At night the sea was brilliant with plankton. When the birds flew away, they lit the darkness with bioluminescence the color of emerald.

On March 18, a moderate northerly wind was blowing. Bernard was able to stop the boat, sails aback, and signal to Cape Town's harbor patrol boat, ELIZABETH R, to approach. He threw onto it a container of film and tapes and spoke for a while with the captain. The latter had little news of the race; he said that four of the competitors had given up, but he didn't know their names. Moitessier wondered if something had happened to his friend Fougeron, or to Bill King, or to Tetley and his vulnerable trimaran.

The ketch picked speed again and approached BRITISH ARGOSY, a small tanker anchored in the bay off Cape Town. A message addressed to the *Sunday Times* and sent by slingshot landed on its deck.

When passed on, this message announcing Moitessier's decision was greeted with amazement, disbelief, and worry. Some people were concerned about the mental health of the sailor after seven months at sea. Alain Glicksmann, editor-in-chief of *Neptune nautisme* magazine, who the year before had sailed in the transatlantic race, wrote that solitude was a dangerous drug that could provoke "an alienation of the personality."

Françoise Moitessier, having made the Tahiti-Alicante voyage, including the rounding of Cape Horn, was well aware of the dangers of the Southern Ocean. Interviewed by the newspaper *L'Aurore*, she admitted being worried. In her radio appeal to Bernard through South Africa Radio, she told him that he was ahead in the race and it was said she also asked him not to undertake a second circumnavigation. However, the next day she denied having sent such a message and said that she fully respected her husband's freedom. The voyage from Polynesia to Spain had exposed her to the magic of the high latitudes and the euphoria that comes with long passages at sea. She understood his decision: "How can I explain my joy in knowing that Bernard continues to live in peace, a free man in the universe he has chosen." To *France-Soir*, the French daily, she admitted: "You can neither advise nor order Bernard. I knew that when I married him."

Moitessier's message, quoted in *L'Aurore* on March 20, 1969, was clear: "I rounded the Horn on February 5 without any damage. Rather than return to England, I am continuing non-stop toward the Pacific Islands." Another message, sent to the commodore of Cape Town Yacht Club, confirmed his decision, as did the short note given to ELIZABETH R asking the French consul to forward a package to Jacques Arthaud: "I am fine physically and mentally."

When this news reached Paris, on March 19, I was traveling in the provinces. I had a full-time job and was freelancing as a nautical journalist. On March 20, *L'Aurore*, one of the newspapers I wrote for, devoted the entire back page to Moitessier's decision. I only had time to dictate a text for the later editions that appeared under the title: *"Moitessier turns his back on the race."* I concluded: "While the parade was being prepared and the band was polishing the brass, Bernard Moitessier in a noble gesture turned his back on anything that could diminish the human value and unselfishness of his achievement."

We had to wait until Saturday, March 22, and the arrival of the package passed on by the French consul to know more. It contained photo negatives, films, and tapes for Jacques Arthaud, Pierre Lavat, the editor of *Bateaux*, and myself. We gathered the next day in Jacques Arthaud's office. Françoise came and listened to his happy, serene voice, coming from so far.

Evidently the solo sailor, after six months of silence, was ready to talk. He said he was in good health, in large part thanks to practicing yoga, which helped him to rediscover the wisdom of the Orient. He confided: "I'm not doing anything. I'm alive, simply, I'm alive." He admitted: "It's not always easy, but when it's beautiful, it's fantastic." He added: "It would be a mistake to return to Europe. That continent is not mine. I've been marked by another civilization." Three decades earlier, Gerbault had expressed the same disenchantment: "My three years of returning to civilization seem empty, totally empty, emptier than a week in an atoll."

Moitessier described at length the technical aspects of his voyage, the perfect condition of the boat and its rigging, and asked that this information be used exclusively by *Bateaux*, the magazine that had published his articles for the last ten years. He asked that a copy of the tapes be given to the *Sunday Times* for publication in Britain. He revealed his intention to head perhaps towards the Galápagos and asked Jacques Arthaud to get him a visa from the Ecuadorian authorities, send letters to the port captains, and, if he anchored in the archipelago, to send him some money, typewriter paper, and whatever he needed to write his book. He also read from his log, adding with a laugh: "If something should happen to me, you have enough material for a book."

Bernard was very wary of the media, in particular some

journalists he thought were second rate. He cared only for a few, in particular one whose name he had forgotten but whom he described as having "fire in his belly." We guessed he meant Philippe Gildas. Bernard asked me to organize a dinner at my house with three or four carefully selected journalists and have them listen to the tapes. While he viewed some of the press with contempt, he contradicted himself by telling Arthaud: "Get the most out of them, don't hold back. Not for the money, I couldn't care less, but for the beauty of it."

His reservations were groundless. The media understood the symbolism of his decision; they gave great play to the fact that he gave up when victory was within reach. The French radio station, RTL, played part of his tapes. *France-Soir* published excerpts from his log. A large number of articles appeared, even in the very serious *Journal de Genève*. Jacques Arthaud negotiated a photo exclusive with *Paris Match*. Monday was the day the weekly wrapped up each issue. I arrived after a full day at work to learn I had to write a long article at once. When I brought my copy in that evening, Françoise was there. She read it, then kissed me: "I didn't realize you knew him that well." In 1987, in one of his letters, Moitessier confirmed that I had understood his decision. "A friend who works at the *Paris Match* archives showed me the article you wrote about me 18 years ago when I was passing by the Cape of Good Hope, bound for the unknown. This article was absolutely remarkable, you reached the heart of the problem." The next issue of *Paris Match* had Moitessier on the cover and eight pages of color photos he had taken during his extraordinary voyage on three oceans.

Although in his log Bernard often mentioned Françoise and the children, the tapes contained no message for her. She received a letter dated March 17, forwarded by the French embassy in South Africa: *"I don't have the courage to come back . . . maybe some day I will return."*[7]

If he had finished the Golden Globe race, in all likelihood as the winner, Bernard Moitessier would have entered the annals as the first sailor to complete a solo non-stop circumnavigation. By turning his back on Europe, on what he called his false gods, he became a guru. The cover of the French edition of Peter Nichols's book about the Golden Globe, *A Voyage for Madmen*, written 30 years later, has neither a photograph of the winner of the race, Knox-Johnston, nor of his boat SUHAILI. It has a picture of Moitessier and JOSHUA and a reproduction of the front page of *L'Aurore* of March 20, 1969 with its headline, "Moitessier renounces an almost certain victory."

Wise, familiar with Asian philosophy, and because he had the courage to say no, Bernard would come to influence a whole generation. Philippe Jeantot who twice won the BOC Challenge, a solo circumnavigation with stops, and went on to organize the Vendée Globe, wrote:" I was 15 when I received as a gift *The Long Way* by Bernard Moitessier. I read it twice the same night and I knew I had found my way."

1, 5. *Tamata and the Alliance.*
2, 3, 6. *The Long Way.*
4. *A World of My Own.*
7. *60,000 Milles à la Voile.*

12

The masts in the water

Five days after Bernard Moitessier's announcement that he wasn't going to Plymouth, Nigel Tetley's VICTRESS rounded Cape Horn. The British naval officer had encountered much trouble. Three weeks prior, his catamaran had been close to sinking. Its fragile structure was damaged: The steering system had failed, a wheelhouse window shattered, and several frames and deck beams cracked. Upon hearing of the Frenchman's decision, Tetley understood he had a good chance of being the fastest around the world. Nothing had been heard from Robin Knox-Johnston since New Zealand and the organizers were becoming increasingly worried.

Crowhurst alone seemed a threat. He had been the last to leave England. According to the positions he gave and the

estimates of his probable average speed, TEIGNMOUTH ELEC-
TRON was now about 3,100 miles from Cape Horn and he
would round it on about April 13, making him a potential
winner of the 5,000 pounds. He had announced a 243-mile
day, an astonishing feat in view of his generally mediocre speed.
Chichester, the most experienced of the observers, didn't be-
lieve him.

Far removed from these concerns, Moitessier went his own
way, enjoying very good weather at first in what he called a
marvelous summer for those latitudes. He resisted the temptation he had for a moment in the bay at Cape Town: a burning
desire to enter the harbor, in search of rest, friends, and the
good times he'd known in the days of MARIE-THÉRÈSE II and his
pal Henry Wakelam. He wasn't sorry he had continued: *"When
I go on deck at dawn, I sometimes shout my joy at being alive,
watching the sky turning white above the long streaks of foam on
this colossally powerful, beautiful sea."*[1]

He had found truth. He was rejecting the materialistic civilization of the West and its constant pursuit of progress, even
as he recognized that technological advances had made possible
his fine boat. His anger gave rise to dreams of an ecological
utopia. Its cities would be more inviting and peaceful: Bicycles
would replace cars, trees would be planted, and birdsong would
be heard.

The fair conditions didn't last. Autumn in the high latitudes lived up to its reputation. I would learn of this later,
when Bernard told me about it. I had agreed with *Paris Match*
that, as soon as JOSHUA reached a port, I would catch the first
plane and meet Moitessier. I had taken the precaution of

obtaining a visa for the Galápagos. When we heard that he had anchored in Tahiti, I found a faster and easier way to interview him. Through the helpful post office staff in Papeete, I was given the phone number of the café closest to the quay. A Tahitian woman with a lilting accent agreed to go find him, and during a long conversation he told me all he had been through in those difficult last weeks.

In the Roaring Forties, starting in early April, which corresponds to October in the Northern Hemisphere, gales follow one after another. East winds, rather unusual in that region, forced Moitessier to heave-to. The staysail, in use from the outset, ripped. He replaced the tired sails with the smaller, stronger ones he had in reserve. When the west winds returned, they blew at storm force. Fleeing under a small jib, JOSHUA was knocked down, her masts in the water. The bad weather battered him relentlessly for two weeks. A second time, an enormous breaking wave rolled the sturdy ketch to the point that her keel was out of the water. The weather improved off Australia and on May 5, he approached Tasmania to signal his presence. He sailed very close to the Hobart lighthouse in squally weather with intermittent gales and calms. This region is beset by reefs and currents and is dangerous for a sailboat without a motor. Moitessier headed offshore without having been seen.

On May 10, after another northwesterly gale, he found himself in dreadful conditions south of New Zealand. In fog, with visibility just one mile, and unable to get a position for two days, he had only his instincts to rely on. This time, the dolphins didn't come to guide him away from danger. En-

couraged by a star sight taken on the fly during a brief clearing, he sailed rather audaciously through the rock-strewn passage between Samres and Auckland Island.

Even if the cold wasn't biting—it was 48°F in the cabin—
salt and dampness permeated the boat, clinging to his clothes
and making every surface sticky to the touch. But despite the
extreme discomfort and the first signs of the austral winter,
Bernard studied the globe with Cape Horn at the far side of the
Pacific and was sorely tempted. Fascinated, beyond all reason,
he thought: "Perhaps one should go further looking at the sea."

In a lucid moment, he realized he was on the edge of exhaustion. He wasn't eating well. He had no energy for cooking,
even if he had the time for it. This meticulous sailor was even
starting to neglect the maintenance of his beloved sailboat.

On May 16, JOSHUA was rolled upside down for the third
time, then again on June 5, when he was at latitude 34° south
and could have expected to have left behind the most dangerous areas. "A northwest gale that turned west, then southwest,
created a confused sea," he told me. "JOSHUA was hit portside
by an enormous breaking wave." The ketch capsized, her keel
almost straight up. Moitessier, who had been in his berth,
found himself pressed against the overhead, wedged under two
mattresses and two heavy sail bags, and crushed by a 30-pound
toolbox ejected from the bilges. The masts—the abandoned
telephone poles that he'd bought because he had little
money—still stood. The outcome could have been worse. He
had to replace four damaged sails and repair three broken
shrouds. The boat was tired, and so was Bernard. He headed
more northeastwards toward quieter latitudes, but he stayed in

the westerlies until he was well past the longitude of Tahiti. When he could sail to Tahiti in following winds, his course was northwest.

At last he found the warm trade wind and he almost cried when he picked up his first flying fish on deck. He had found the favorable breezes beloved by sailors. For 16 days he rested, slept, ate, and let the tropical sun reinvigorate his tired body.

On the morning of June 21, the red ketch entered the pass at Papeete and reached the roadstead that's protected by two outer reefs. The cruisers moored along the quay noticed the red, rust-streaked hull and the stretched, gray sails. One of them shouted: "Moitessier! It's Moitessier!"

After 10 months at sea, almost to the day, the sailor, thin, tanned, with a long gray beard, unkempt hair, prominent muscles, and wearing an old pair of shorts, dropped the anchor and threw a line. Among those who took the line were Pierre Deshumeurs, his old friend from SNARK, and other friends Bernard had met by chance in various ports of call. They came on board.

JOSHUA was motionless for the first time after 300 days at sea. And Bernard, the solo sailor, told tale after tale in the precious warmth of people and friendship and the wonderful aroma of coffee and cigarettes.

---

1. *The Long Way.*

13

---⊶⊷⊷⊶---

Royalties for the Pope

While Moitessier made his long way through the autumnal storms of the Indian Ocean, Robin Knox-Johnston completed his voyage. On April 12, a cargo ship spotted SUHAILI near the Azores. On April 22, Knox-Johnston, dogged, courageous, sailed the ketch into Falmouth after 313 days at sea. As he had hoped, it was indeed an Englishman who won the solo non-stop race around the world. Knox-Johnston was knighted by the queen and became Sir Robin.

Nigel Tetley was hoping to be the fastest, but he felt threatened by Crowhurst whose TEIGNMOUTH ELECTRON looked like a possible winner. In spite of the trimaran's sorry condition, Tetley decided to push his luck. The boat's condition deteriorated until it broke up in a gale and sank near the Azores, almost within reach of the finish. A tanker rescued Tetley the next day.

As for Crowhurst, if the positions he had given were true, he would win both fame and money, but Chichester, to whom his messages had been relayed, suspected a hoax. On July 10, the officer of the watch on a cargo ship, PICARDY, spotted a trimaran adrift. Sent to board the deserted craft, Joseph Clark, the first mate, found two logs. One revealed an imaginary voyage while the other recorded the actual route. Crowhurst had never left the Atlantic Ocean. The last position was dated July 1. Donald Crowhurst had put an end to his deception.

———— ✺ ————

After JOSHUA left Plymouth, Françoise abandoned the house in Bandol and moved to Mantes, near Paris. A woman doctor was opening a practice in electroencephalography and offered her both a position and an apartment. As soon as Bernard arrived in Papeete, Jean-Pierre Aymon, editor in chief of *France-Soir* and a cruiser himself, took her to Tahiti. Her husband was not the yogi in the pictures taken when he tied up after 10 months at sea. He had cut his hair and his beard and was freshly shaven—he was impeccable. "We met again. It was very emotional; we were very nervous but also deliriously happy," she said. Françoise had to go back to her job in France. Bernard promised her: *"While I'm writing the book, you will take care of the films in Paris and within a year, we'll be through with both and be able to leave again."*[1] Strangely enough, Bernard never mentioned their reunion in any of his writings.

Two years passed. The relationship between the two entered a very different phase. The sailor probably wanted to prolong the solitude he'd known on the ocean. The bonds with his wife, about whom he'd spoken with great tenderness after Tahiti-Alicante, were loosening. *"We had chosen different paths."*[2]

In 1970, Tabarly entered the Los Angeles-Tahiti race. Alain Colas also decided to enter and chartered a sailboat, NARRA-GANSETT. Françoise joined the crew as a way to see her husband again and perhaps to get them back together. But the welcome she received on board JOSHUA left her in no doubt.

In Tahiti, courtesy of the French Navy, JOSHUA was cleaned up and had her bottom scrubbed. Moitessier could start writing *The Long Way*. In the tapes he sent from the Cape of Good Hope, he had asked Jacques Arthaud to reserve this title for the story about his voyage.

But the hero of the Golden Globe was much less comfortable facing a blank page than confronting the gales of the Southern Ocean. The story of his voyage could not be a simple rewrite of the log. It had to evoke the magnitude of his quest for an absolute truth and explain his decision to those who still did not understand. Alain Glicksman was one of them. For him, an offshore racer, the sole reason to enter a race was to win. Bernard tried to get him to see his point: "I emerge from the water after swimming over half a mile along the coral reef. To me, this is just as moving as a triumphal entrance into Plymouth."

When he signed the contract with his publisher, Moitessier

had assumed that he would have the manuscript ready six months after his return. But he realized: *"Ten months alone on a boat making her way between sky and sea is something that can hardly be expressed in all its fullness. This voyage, both physical and spiritual, was made up of gestures that were too simple and feelings that were too intense to be expressed in our poor, everyday words."*[3]

He wrote to me for help, "Try to give me as clear an outline as possible, emphasizing the principal points. If you can put some serious effort into balancing and completing this outline, I'm pretty sure I'll be able to flesh it out well enough."

In a very long letter dated September 19, 1969, I tried to help him loosen up so he could get started, He replied by return mail. "I'm working at it full-time, with ups and downs." Writing *The Long Way* demanded a supreme effort from him.

In between, Moitessier allowed himself some time off. In 1969 Eric Tabarly arrived on his 67-foot trimaran, PEN DUICK IV, accompanied by crewmembers Olivier de Kersauson, Jean-Michel Carpentier, and Alain Colas. Side by side lay a primitive steel boat as solid as a safe and a futuristic ultra-light aluminum boat that looked like a dragonfly. Of their skippers, one was a sailor-philosopher in search of the truth and the other a broad-backed, muscular Breton on a quest for speed and victory. The two men had never met. After the official reception for the winner of the transatlantic race that Tabarly couldn't avoid, the two sailors would be found on one or the other of their boats, entertaining each other with their disparate views.

At that time, Tabarly was thinking of sailing solo around

the world against the prevailing winds. He was interested in Moitessier's experience in the Southern Ocean. He marveled at JOSHUA's comfortable and simple interior with its curtains that Françoise had made to cover the portholes, its library full of books, and its wide berths. Moitessier was in awe of PEN DUICK IV, a boat technically ahead of its time, with an abundance of winches, a sophisticated rig, battened sails, and instrumentation that seemed more appropriate in the cockpit of a fighter plane rather than a luxury yacht. Alain Colas, camera in hand and notebook at the ready, was an attentive witness whenever these two sailors met. He wrote an article about them in *Neptune nautisme*. Kersauson, too, wrote down every word and sent a story to *Paris Match*.

Bernard gave me his opinion about Tabarly's proposal to sail against the prevailing winds, "His project is fantastic. I don't know what to think. It seems to me impossible to sail all the way around the world south of the fortieth parallel, beating to windward from east to west. As for trying to take advantage of the few easterlies by going down to 60° south. . . ." He advised Eric to equip his future boat with a bowsprit, and gave him a few tips: Put old newspapers on the cabin sole to absorb the damp, wear long underwear to keep warm, and take rubber boots because canvas ones never dry. He told him to practice yoga.

Moitessier joined Tabarly and his crewmembers for a cruise to the Society Islands aboard MAYLIS, a superb 67-foot traditional ketch. Her owner, Marc Darnois, was a war hero, who'd lost a leg fighting the Japanese and now was using his considerable charm to develop publicity for Polynesia. The cruise was a success. Eric, biceps bulging and a tiare flower over his ear, and Bernard, spare and wiry, sweated the halyards and sheeted home the jib. Moitessier enthralled his shipmates with the warmth of his friendship and tales of his childhood in Indochina and his life as a vagabond. They were amazed how lithe he was and how adroitly he could hold a packet of tobacco between his toes and roll a cigarette with one hand.

When he heard what de Kersauson had written in *Paris Match* to accompany his photos, however, Bernard was outraged. Olivier had called him a hippie. On November 27, 1969, he addressed a long letter to the weekly magazine, taking exception to the term.

> I'm not sure that a hippie can run a sailing school, make films and pictures, write books and specialized articles . . .
> For the world at large, the word "hippie" implies drugs and laziness. I never took drugs, unless smoking a packet of tobacco in three days qualifies, and I'm no lazier than the average person.

He worried that Françoise's children might be hurt should their schoolmates taunt them with, "Your father is a hippie," implying he was a drug-taking, lazy, ne'er do well. He was also upset that de Kersauson had dared to describe JOSHUA as out of date and he defended the qualities of his ketch, built as it was for safe and comfortable cruising, not for racing. In fact, Jean Knocker's design gave rise to a series of boats that Fricaud built. In 1971, Françoise informed me in a letter that the forty-first hull had just been launched.

At the end of 1969, Bernard spent a few weeks in France in total secrecy. Though his publisher asked him to attend the Salon Nautique, he refused. He went to ground in Françoise's apartment in Mantes. We were invited for dinner and spent an emotional evening by the fireplace. Then Bernard left for Tahiti and Françoise wrote to us. "I go on trying to live here and it seems to me more and more difficult."

The images filmed during *the long way* had extraordinary power and beauty, a remarkable achievement for someone who had never used a camera before. Bernard asked Françoise to make the most out of the film. After meticulous editing, the film was ready to be screened at the Salle Pleyel. Françoise told me she was nervous about having to introduce it.

October 5, 1971

> I must tell you that I am more and more scared, first of all because I'm not a good public speaker, and second, because I feel completely abandoned by Bernard. I was hoping he would come back to France for a few days, happy to see his book in print and his film on the screen.

She had written to him but he didn't reply. Françoise, a very small figure on the stage of this huge hall, found it hard not to show her emotion, despite the presence of friends there to support her. The event was a great success. Other screenings took place all over France and in Switzerland and Belgium, with Françoise presenting all of them. The film, produced with the help of Jean-Marie Perthuis, won second prize at the festival of films of the sea and exploration in Toulon. I continued to exchange letters with Bernard.

March 22, 1970

I read yesterday, and again today, your article in *Neptune*. You said exactly what needed to be said. You felt that one person had accomplished something universal and you expressed it well. I sent Chapter 10 (Good Hope) to Arthaud. Let me know what you think. I'm very isolated and sometimes I get discouraged. Chapter 11 has been under way for a month . . . I'm not finished because it's so difficult. I'm working hard but I'm up against it with this damn chapter.

Among the books Moitessier read and reread during his circumnavigation and a half was Romain Gary's *The Roots of Heaven*. I bought another of Gary's books and went to visit him in the apartment Gallimard let him use on rue du Bac. After autographing the book, he gave me yet another book for Moitessier. I sent the books to Papeete where Bernard continued to have trouble writing.

September 8

Thank you for the two novels by Romain Gary . . . I am at a loss for the moment and I'm afraid this might last quite a while if I don't get some help . . . I don't know whom to turn to except for you.

September 30

I didn't answer right away because that damn chapter was driving me crazy (Chapter 18–Time to Choose) and it practically exhausted me. I'm enclosing here confidentially a first try, and a second, shorter version. I sent Arthaud a third version. This chapter is extremely hard to write. There is a very fine line between the sublime and the absurd.

October 25

I flew to an atoll to get some rest, but I don't have a much clearer idea. Don't worry, I'll get there in the end. I don't yet know how.

By the summer of 1971, to the author's great relief, the hard work of writing was almost done. *"It took two years of misery, but also indescribable joys, to recreate in* The Long Way *what I felt was a faithful reflection of the incredible journey . . . Substantial royalties would soon be coming my way. The jackpot! And with that, no more worries for the rest of my days!"*[4]

All of a sudden, at the point of sending his manuscript, Moitessier had an epiphany. He wanted to give his message an ultimate dimension. He wrote to his publisher that his domestic and foreign royalties were to be paid to the Pope. In *Tamata and the Alliance* he explained this surprising decision. *"The Long Way* had to carry the same weight as the voyage. Accepting my royalties would amount to denying myself, to implicitly erasing the entire passage all the way from Plymouth."

With this spectacular and symbolic gesture, Moitessier wanted to emphasize the concern that all mankind should have to save the planet, to be part of the creation of the world, not of its destruction. He wanted to shout that the Western world was heading in the wrong direction. The mission of a new organization, the Friends of the World, would be to ensure that the Vatican used this money "to help to rebuild the world."

One of the founders of the organization, Alain Hervé, a journalist, had sailed with his wife and his cousin Bernard Pichard, from France to Tahiti on his sailboat AVENTURE at the same time that Bernard and Françoise made that voyage. Editions Arthaud published Alain Hervé's book, *Au Vent d'AVENTURE (AVENTURE in the Wind)* in January 1970. He then became involved with ecological movements and became the editor of *Le Sauvage* review. He seemed to Bernard the right person to ask.

The Long Way was published in October 1971. In the last chapter, he wrote that the royalties he rendered to the Pope symbolize "the little flame of spirituality that still flickers in corners of the West."

⸺◦⦿◦⸺

The message that the Golden Globe competitor had delivered in Cape Town Bay, announcing that he was continuing nonstop "to save his soul," had created a big uproar in the media. Bernard thought that renouncing his royalties would also find a huge echo.

But nothing happened. His gesture was met with silence

and total indifference. Jacques Arthaud told the Grenoble diocese about this windfall for the Vatican. Two years after publication, the money was still with the publisher. Neither the Vatican nor Friends of the Earth had seen fit to take advantage of the gift they'd received, nor did they show the least interest in the message Bernard wanted to communicate. *"I hadn't expected such a complete defeat, such a dead calm after my attempt to shake up people's consciences."*[5]

He'd been betrayed by his naïveté. The media gave his generous gesture none of the coverage he'd hoped for. To give up glory in the middle of the ocean during the most pitiless solo voyage contained all the romantic ingredients that would pique the press and spark the popular imagination. But it was a different story for an author, even Moitessier, to give up his royalties, even to the Pope, under the delusion that he could help save the planet. This complicated message couldn't be explained in sound bites. Why would anyone working hard to make ends meet understand the slightly crazy initiative of a sailor who spent his days peacefully under the tropical sun?

The sailor-writer was disappointed. Moreover, he now suffered the after effects of the vast tiredness caused by 10 months alone in the Southern Ocean and the subsequent labor of writing his book. He was entering an even more difficult period: a time of doubt.

———— ⚭ ————

1. *60,000 Milles à la Voile.*
2, 3, 4, 5. *Tamata and the Alliance.*

14

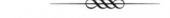

The hippie years

The world was changing, and not always for the better. Because of the nuclear testing in the Pacific, Tahiti was flooded with a wave of modernization. The military and the scientists brought a lot of money and a new way of life. Papeete, once a sleepy, tranquil village full of charm and ease was turning into a town just like any other, with cars, traffic jams, and noise. The earth and stone quay, where the inter-island schooners and the occasional yacht in transit tied up, gave way to concrete. The lovely wooden colonial houses lining the seafront with their boutiques, bistros, and small restaurants were replaced one after another with large uninspiring buildings. The trees shading the street were sacrificed to a wide four-lane road.

Moitessier thought this "yielding to progress" outrageous.

The May 1968 student revolution in France was a brutal reaction against the establishment. It arose shortly after the appearance in the United States of the hippie movement. In the western world, ecological movements were growing. For some, it became trendy to move to the countryside to raise goats and make goat cheese. Others built sailboats, hoping to lead an idle, carefree life in far away islands.

The builders of the future had now caught up with the sailors who'd hoped to escape the rat race and the trappings of the western world in Tahiti. They had been living peacefully aboard their sailboats, gamming at night under the shade of the *pandanus*. Now they were subjected to the dust and rumble of bulldozers, and were witnessing the felling of the trees that shaded them from the sun.

Following the initiative of Moitessier, the most famous among them, they sent a letter of protest to the authorities. "It's not too late to improve the inhuman quay that has been imposed on us," they wrote. For lack of a better solution, they created a small garden near the water to isolate themselves as much as possible from the noise of the street. They planted banana trees and brought in pieces of turf. They often gathered at dusk near the "monkey wrench" (as they called General de Gaulle's monument at the end of the quay), to talk, to put the world to rights. But they didn't just drink from coconuts. Bernard wrote: *"Until I was finished with my writing project, I had carefully resisted the temptation of the marijuana that was being passed around on the quay . . . The marijuana went round and round and I was rarely the last one of the bunch to grab a joint of this herb, with its flavor of the East."*[1]

In *The Long Way*, Moitessier said: "I dream of the day when a country of the modern world has an intensely simple president and barefoot ministers. I'd ask for citizenship right away." Bernard was perfectly true to himself in adopting the legitimate cause of those who disagreed with the "physical and spiritual depradations of the race for Progress."

The local council of Papeete listened in part to the complaints of the port users. The four-lane road was lined with trees, and gardens and lawns were created between it and the quay. Nevertheless the Papeete of before, that of the early sailors of the twentieth century, Gerbault, Le Toumelin, and also of Moitessier on his first visit, was gone.

<hr />

In May 1970 a young woman approached Bernard. Her name was Iléana, and she had just arrived from Guadeloupe. Her father was Roumanian and her mother French. She was traveling around the world and carried in her meager luggage volumes of poetry: Verlaine, Rimbaud, Baudelaire . . .

When she was in Pointe-à-Pitre, she had met Henry Wakelam who had taken on an incredible challenge. He had bought a wrecked 130-foot boat and was hard at work refloating it, fixing it up, and fitting it out. Iléana hoped to go to Australia to find work. Henry suggested she stop in Tahiti and visit his friend Bernard. Henry had an ulterior motive. He had a bit of the devil in him—it was no accident he named his new boat LUCIFER. Two years later, he said to me with a laugh: "I knew she was Bernard's type."

When Moitessier met Iléana, he was writing the last chapters of his book. She found a small *faré* near the lagoon, a bicycle ride from JOSHUA. Bernard repaired the roof, settled into the house, and pedaled every morning to his boat to scribble a few more pages. Very soon his companion was pregnant. But Bernard and Iléana were well aware of the precariousness of their relationship. *"I told her that I would always need my freedom."*[2]

Iléana had understood from the first day. Her pregnancy, at first a surprise, slowly became a precious promise for the father-to-be. Iléana had no money and made her living doing odd jobs. If her companion, as was predictable, were to leave her and the child for God knows what new adventure, what would happen to her? While he was finishing his book and contemplating offering his royalties to the Pope, Bernard had a pang of conscience and wondered if he had the right to deprive the mother and his child of that money.

One evening, ready to send the last chapter, Bernard asked her whether he should accept the security offered by the royalties or take a jump into the unknown. Iléana's reaction was unambiguous. *"To think that I was so proud to be carrying your baby! And here you are turning tail at the first real fight."*[3] The next day, he mailed the last chapter. With it was a note for Arthaud: "Give my royalties to the Pope."

On October 3, 1971, Iléana gave birth to twins. One died two days later. The other, Stephan, survived after 40 days in an incubator. Bernard became an affectionate father, trying to bring up "the child of man" in the image of the hero of *The Jungle Book*, one of his favorite books. In due course, he would make him a slingshot.

In an eight-page letter to Françoise, he told her about meeting Iléana and having a son. Whether it was out of thoughtlessness or innocence, he had the nerve to ask her to send baby clothes he couldn't find in Tahiti. Françoise had to admit: *"My relationship with Bernard was lost with the passing of time."*[4]

In Papeete, under its eternal tropical softness, the years passed without anyone paying attention. Bernard kept busy doing little more than watching his child grow, helping his friend Jesus build a boat, and recreating the world while smoking joints.

———— ∞∞∞ ————

For some time Bernard and I had been at odds. I had let him know that I disagreed with some of his positions. I had also told him that I disapproved of his attitude toward the media. Except for the few he liked, he had bad-mouthed journalists in the tapes he sent off Cape Town. "The media are a bunch of losers." This was both unfair and indiscriminate. Besides, while loudly claiming to despise them, Moitessier wasn't unhappy to have the papers or the radio talking about him. His publisher had managed to sell his photos to *Paris Match*, excerpts from his tapes to the radio station RTL, and excerpts from his log to *France Soir* for high fees, and he didn't turn down the royalties due him. He should not have overlooked the fact that the fame he earned through all this publicity helped sell his books. Anyway, there it was, we were on bad terms. Bernard wrote to me:

June 26, 1971

Here's what we're going to do, the two of us. We both heave-to, we wait until the book comes out. We'll see then which way the wind is blowing, and things will fall back into place without explanation (I mean, neither of us will need an explanation).

Our mutual silence lasted almost six months. I sent him a very long letter on December 2, concluding with these words:

I am not trying to defend our little friends from the media—the press, radio, and TV. First they are quite capable of doing it themselves. But you have to do them justice. Facing your decision, your philosophical positions, and ignoring all the insults you threw at them, they had enough brain to understand the meaning of your decisions and showed enough class to paint them in a flattering way, trying to convince a public, dismayed and reticent at first, that Moitessier was a man who was sincere, lucid, and sympathetic. You can tell me that you couldn't care less, but we both know deep down that this is not true.

———— ⌘ ————

Bernard roamed around Papeete barefoot, wearing a washed out pair of shorts, an old straw hat hiding his face. One would have thought that having finished his book, he would fit out the ketch and go back to the sea he loved. Instead, he seemed to be living aimlessly, not sailing any more, and also neglecting JOSHUA. The sailboat was a sorry sight with rust streaks down her faded paint and her cordage gray with dirt. Would Moitessier, a sailing legend, spend the rest of his life rolling joints, interminably discussing the future of the world with a group of buddies?

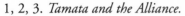

1, 2, 3. *Tamata and the Alliance.*
4. *60,000 Milles à la Voile.*

15

Suvorov, the magic atoll

It was high time that Moitessier realized idle talk and joints weren't going to get him very far. The sailor who during his long way had brushed the "fourth dimension" and glimpsed the temple hidden in the forest, continued his quest after he had finished writing his book.

In order to give depth to the unending conversations at the quay, to achieve wisdom, and to understand the universe, this one-time dunce read with the voraciousness of the self-taught. Nearing 50, he wanted to study all the philosophy. He read Confucius, Lao Tse, Lanza del Vasto, René Guénon, Sri Aurobindo, Gurdjieff, and many others who he hoped would provide answers to his questions. He continued to doubt and was near depression.

Salvation came in one name, Suvorov. Suvorov was, for all sorts of reasons, "magical," a term that Moitessier used often in his writings. Part of the Cook Islands, 200 miles from the nearest inhabited island, half way between Tahiti and Samoa, the atoll is far from shipping lanes and is rarely visited. It is, nevertheless, one of the most beautiful places on earth.

The lagoon is 50 miles in circumference and protected by a reef and *motus*—islets that form on top of reefs. The discoverers of this atoll lacked imagination when they named its principal features. The pass that gives easy access to the lagoon has a beacon in the middle consisting of a rock named Entrance Island. The main island, about half a mile long, where the rare visitors anchor, is Anchorage Island. In the northeast are seven islets named Seven Islands.

In 1952 a New Zealander and former sailor, Tom Neale, at the age of 50, decided to live on this deserted island as a hermit. He stayed there almost without interruption for a quarter of a century until 1977 when cancer forced him to leave for Rarotonga, where he later died.

Throughout his lonely sojourn, Tom Neale had to work very hard to survive on an atoll poor in natural resources. He dug the earth to create a garden, made a chicken coop, fished, and built and rebuilt the jetty which was regularly destroyed by cyclones. Above all, he developed his own philosophy of life. Tom Neale didn't talk much but he made his points by acting on them. His book about his experiences, *An Island to Oneself: Six Years on a Desert Island,* was published in 1966.

Such a character, and the way he participated in the creation of the world, could not but fascinate Moitessier. In his periods of doubt, which he went through several times, Bernard always sought out guides and tried to meet exceptional characters. In Indochina it was the fishermen of the Gulf of Siam, Assam, his Chinese amah, and Abadie. In South Africa, it was Wakelam. Soon, it would be Phil, an Israeli passing through Tahiti, who told him: "Sooner or later, the truth seeker finds a 'master' on his path."

When Bernard awoke from his period of idleness, he made a swift decision. He had to flee Papeete and its sapping atmosphere. First he had to put JOSHUA back in shape. For three years he had neglected her, and a steel boat doesn't forgive poor maintenance. Chipping away the rust, painting, making good the rigging, and repairing the sails, took almost a year of work.

At last, in 1973, the family headed for New Zealand where Bernard and Iléana hoped to find a climate and society more suited to their intellectual life and in which Stephan could thrive. On board were Bernard, Iléana, Stephan, almost two, and Miguel, a capable American crew who'd fallen in love with the boat. Suvorov was almost on the route and it became a matter of urgency to visit the magical atoll, meet its hermit, and discover his truth.

From the moment he arrived in Suvorov, Bernard was dazzled. He wrote an afterword to the French edition of Tom Neale's book.

"Suvorov became a magical atoll. There in all simplicity with his hands, his conscience and his courage, with his magical shovel and his magical machete, with his sweat and his love, a man had participated in the creation of the world."

JOSHUA stayed in Suvorov for three months. The boat lay

at anchor most of the time off a motu that Bernard and Iléana named Bird Island because of the colonies of terns that nested there. With machetes, crowbars, shovels, and picks, Bernard and Miguel cleared the earth, thinned the undergrowth, and planted 130 germinated coconuts to start a coconut grove.

That is when Moitessier made an astonishing discovery: there was fresh water on the atoll. He had dug a pit on Bird Island and the water that seeped in at the bottom was fresh. He explained the phenomenon much later in an article on March 1988 in *Neptune-yachting.* "At first, it would seem that there can't be water on an atoll . . . But there, without fanfare, a small miracle said 'no' to big old commonsense. During the rainy season water from the sky penetrates the sand to gently overlay that from the sea. Fresh water is lighter than saltwater so it floats on top."

The sojourn in New Zealand didn't live up to Bernard's expectations. "I was turning in circles. I didn't know what to do with my life." Iléana encouraged him to go to Israel. Once again Stephan's mother showed what an extraordinary woman she was. Ignoring her own needs, she always gave him the right advice at the right time. Just as she'd encouraged Bernard to renounce his royalties, even if it meant living in poverty, without a second thought, though she had never sailed before, she boarded JOSHUA for the passage to Suvorov and New Zealand. She accepted now to stay behind with her son and said to Bernard. "Phil is a wise man. He has invited you to live in his commune. Go join him. You might find some answers."

Moitessier stopped over in Paris. He asked his publisher to give him the royalties the Vatican had failed to collect. Over three years, the book had sold more than 100,000 copies. The author was suddenly rich. He wasn't flush for long, however. Although he was frugal, his only resources were his royalties. In Polynesia where everything was expensive, he was supporting a family and a boat, and the money dried up very quickly. He wrote to me:

September 21, 1974

I'm in France for another few weeks and I would love to see you and Dany. But under one condition: that your name is only Jean-Michel, let's ignore your last name. In other words, I want to see you as a friend, not as a journalist. Affectionately.

On meeting Bernard at Arthaud, I asked him to come and have dinner with us. Dany was painting her mother's apartment at the time and I called her to let her know. Here a funny thing happened. We were living on the fifth (and last) floor of a very chic apartment building on Avenue Marceau. Dany abandoned her painting and went shopping for dinner. She bought a cake at a pastry shop near our home and forgot it. Noticing that she'd forgotten it, she went back to the pastry shop where she was told that it had been delivered to our apartment. Dany then saw the delivery man who said: "I left your cake." He added then, with a strange look, "Your guest has arrived already." Dany found Bernard lying on the landing, barefoot, his head on a sail bag, He explained: "One should never miss out on the opportunity to get some rest."

Moitessier stayed for two and a half months in Israel, in the small commune Phil had started. *"I was at a complete dead end in my life. I had to go to Jerusalem. It was my last hope."*[1] After Assam, Abadie, and Tom Neale, Phil was the new master who came to help him confront his perpetual despair. The regimen in the commune was strict. Rise at 4 a.m., meditations at dawn, write up a journal. These spiritual exercises and the teachings inspired by Gurdjieff were followed by manual work in the gardens, intense physical activity in which he was constantly aware of his actions.

Before leaving Israel, Bernard traveled through the desert with a group of pilgrims and climbed Mount Sinaï. *"Among my companions hungry for God and miracles, I noticed a beautiful woman of twenty-two."*[2] She had done some sailing and had read *The Long Way*, which she thought wonderful. She joyfully accepted Bernard's invitation to explore the bays of New Zealand aboard JOSHUA.

Over the course of six months, the seeker of truth traveled in France, stayed in Israel, and, in Hong Kong, rediscovered the smells of the Orient. During his short stay in France he visited Jacques-Yves Le Toumelin in Brittany. The two sailors hardly talked about boats and sailing around the world but discussed the direction the world was taking. Le Toumelin, too, was looking for a sense of spirituality, and was influenced by Buddhism, which his sister practiced.

Iléana and Stephan had to leave New Zealand because their visas weren't renewed. After cruising the northeast coast of New Zealand, Moitessier brought JOSHUA back to Tahiti, in 23 days. *"An exceptional passage. Eighteen days around the 37th parallel without once dropping the genoa, with quite a few calms toward the end of the trip."*[3]

On April 10, 1975, the red ketch anchored off the "monkey wrench." Two months later, Dany and I arrived in Tahiti, on our way from Panama on a new sailboat we were delivering for a French couple who lived in Polynesia. As a journalist writing for *Le Figaro* and *Paris Match*, a senior editor of *Voiles et Voiliers* and co-publisher of the Sea series at Editions Arthaud, I couldn't stay away from my work for more than two months and our stay in Papeete was short. In Arué, near the yacht club, we found Bernard sewing hanks on a staysail for his friend Jesus, and we met Iléana and Stephan, aged four, for the first time.

Bernard had just turned 50. Life went on, apparently peacefully. Iléana had found a faré not too far from the harbor and she was making beautiful *pareus* that were sold in the stores. Bernard was tending to JOSHUA's tired sails, sewing them by hand, watching his son grow up, wondering about his future and worrying about where the world was going.

A young man of 22, Dominique Charnay, a journalist at *La Dépêche de Tahiti*, found the nerve to interview Moitessier. A friendship began between the two men that would continue in Paris, until Bernard's death. A talented photographer, Charnay took a series of portraits of the sailor and described his special relationship with the sailor-philosopher in a beautifully illustrated book, *Moitessier, le chemin des îles.*

Six months went by. The sojourn in Israel and Phil's teachings brought no answer to Bernard's question, "What should I do with my life?" He felt the need to return to Suvorov. He would bring Tom some provisions and a new machete and give him a hand. He would find out how the coconut trees he'd planted on Bird Island were doing, and chase away his doubts with sweat. The atoll fascinated Moitessier and he went there six times between 1973 and 1985. When he arrived in 1976, he felt like a lover rejoining his beloved. He told Jean Knocker that it was a fantastic trip, in the company of a 25-year-old beauty.

A big disappointment was in store for him on Bird Island. Of the 130 coconut trees he had planted, only five had survived. Undeterred, he cleared the *tahinus* (messerschmidia argentea) that had choked the sprouted nuts and planted 50 new coconut trees. With the help of Tom and his formidable determination, he tried to recover his serenity. *"Coming to Suvorov I hadn't known what to think. I am not sure that Bird Island completely answered my question. But one thing is certain: I would never give up on the great love affair between Man and Creation."*[4]

Only eleven days remained because his crew had to fly back to Paris: her vacation was over. The passage that had taken six days in following winds coming took two weeks of beating into the trade winds going back. But he called it a great sail.

As he'd promised, he was back in Tahiti just in time to celebrate Stephan's birthday. His son's future worried him. His one thought for him and for the rest of humanity was to seek paths that led to true wisdom.

1, 2, 3, 4. *Tamata and the Alliance.*

16

Utopia in Ahé

In October 1975, Moitessier wrote to Jean Knocker from Tahiti:

> Dear Uncle Jean
>
> I am now planning to move to Ahé, an atoll in the Tuamotus located 240 miles northeast of Tahiti. Iléana and Stephan spent three weeks there while I was sailing, and Iléana seemed to think it was a good spot for Stephan.
>
> The decision to move to Ahé was based on several factors. First, Ahé would be a nice place for Stephan to grow up, close to nature. It was a medium-sized, very beautiful atoll. The

entrance pass to the superb lagoon became even easier of access for Bernard thanks to a 10-hp diesel engine recently installed on JOSHUA. A coral outcropping off the main island formed a natural shelter and a small jetty permitted boats to come alongside if they didn't draw too much. The population of 80, which included 30 children, was friendly. The prospect pleased Iléana, too.

In Ahé, removed from Papeete's lifestyle, Bernard wanted to apply the methods he'd picked up from Tom Neale in Suvorov and from Phil in his commune at Ein Kerem. Talking to Charnay in Papeete, he had derided the demands for autonomy being made by the local politicians. "True independence starts with feeding yourself. In Polynesia the authorities are always talking about large economic and social projects, but I never heard a word about agriculture. And in the meantime the Polynesians do not produce the food they eat."

Moitessier intended to show by example that on the reputedly sterile soil of an atoll you could grow vegetables and plant mango and avocado trees. Gathering coconuts and harvesting copra was the only source of income for the atolls. He hoped that if the inhabitants, the Paumotus, could diversify their crops and increase their production, they could be induced to stay home instead of becoming unemployed layabouts in Papeete. Alain Gerbault had mentioned this idea in his book *Islands of Beauty*, "From time to time earth is brought to the Nirihu atoll and deposited in large pits dug in the middle of the coral. Here, a few breadfruit and orange trees grow and supplement the food rations. This is laudable and should be encouraged. These islands should be able to produce more food."

Bernard promoted this new crusade with the ardor of an evangelist. Helped by a sailor friend, Luciano Lavadas, he salvaged planks and beams abandoned by the Tahiti yacht club. Cut to the right size, they would form the skeleton of his future faré. He loaded them onto JOSHUA, and then made a laborious upwind passage. He told the story in a letter to a friend, November 15, 1975.

> On the deck was all the wood necessary to frame the floors of two small farés. We will live in one of them (18 feet x 12 feet on stilts). The other faré will be the workshop where Iléana will do her sewing (12 feet x 9 feet, also on stilts). The forepeak was stuffed with planks cut in half for the two farés. There was also a ton of topsoil in gunny bags on the cabin sole, plus anything you can imagine we'd need to live on an atoll, among other things, six sacks of cement.

The ketch, now transformed into a cargo ship, also carried rolls of wire mesh, lemon and mango trees in pots, seeds . . .

Once through the pass, JOSHUA entered the magic of the atolls: *"After the open ocean swell, it was wonderful to crisscross this beautiful calm, blue water in every direction, to make love to this lagoon which had seduced me from the very first moment."*[1] Poro Poro is a motu about an acre in area facing the anchorage. A coral isthmus connecting it to the village makes it a sort of peninsula. Bernard dreamt of creating a commune, like Ein Kerem.

On one half of the motu lived a couple, Patrick, a Frenchman, Diana, an American, and their two children, aged 5 and 7 who would be friends for Stephan. Patrick had fallen in love with Ahé and started a small business transporting fish on his 50-foot sailboat, which he'd fitted with a refrigerated hold. The Paumotus helped him build a faré with traditional material. They lived there happily until the day he lost his boat on the reef while loading fish. Now, Patrick and Diana were thinking of leaving for Tahiti. At the same time, the villagers allowed Bernard and Iléana to settle on Poro Poro.

After a few days of very hard work, with the help of Patrick and Luciano, who had come on his own boat, GUIA, the house was finished. It was built of local material, on stilts, four feet off the ground. Next to it was a workshop where Iléana could design and sew the pareus she had such a gift for making. *"I now know that it's possible to build a traditional faré on a deserted atoll, using only a machete and a sharpening stone."*[2]

The house that they built, covered with palm fronds woven by Mama Fana and Mama Tehua, was cool and well ventilated, in contrast to the houses now preferred by the villagers which Bernard found upsetting. Instead of the farés that cost nothing and were ideally suited to the tropical climate, the Paumotus built houses of cement block or plywood, with glazed windows, and corrugated-iron roofs that turned them into saunas. All the material had to be imported to Tahiti and then transported at extra cost by the island schooner, which made these houses very expensive.

Bernard was intent on showing that he could live on the food he grew on the atoll. With guidance from Patrick, he built a fish pen in front of Poro Poro. He started a vegetable garden in a tiny bed of soil enclosed by dried palm fronds. The first seeds he planted were watermelons, cucumbers, and pumpkins. Tomato and papaya seedlings would be next. To develop this vegetable garden he needed fertilizer. They began a compost pile with rotting vegetable matter, chicken manure, leftover fish, and, most important, human waste. He had learned this recipe in Indochina and it produced a miraculous fertilizer—"dynamite," Bernard called it. Digging into the soil of Poro Poro, he reached a pocket of fresh water. With regular watering, the garden had a chance.

Luciano and his girlfriend, Patrick and Diana left, but a month after arriving there, Bernard and Iléana were comfortable in their faré. At dusk, they would stroll hand in hand around their domain. *"An infinite, otherworldly tenderness enveloped Poro Poro . . . We didn't know what the earthly paradise that man had lost was like. We could recreate it here, right beneath our feet, by bringing out the god within all of us from the depths of our being, giving this desert the sweat of our bodies and the breath of our souls."*[3]

The lesson Moitessier wanted to apply was that one should set aside habits and prejudices and try. He used the word "try" so often when talking to Ahé's inhabitants, that they called him "Tamata," which means, "to try."

Bernard wrote at length about his 18-month experience in Ahé in his book *Tamata and the Alliance*, and in letters, in particular a 38-page missive to Jean Knocker on June 17, 1978, in which he outlined the lessons learned from living on the atoll. Coming to the Sunday meeting of the village carrying a 40-pound watermelon, he proved that in this supposedly sterile soil, vegetables could grow and fruit trees could prosper. "The Polynesian custom is to burn all the dry palm fronds and other vegetal waste so that the soil gets poorer." Leaving the palm fronds to rot would create compost ready for cultivation. He tried to convince the villagers, using pictures and comparisons, but except for two of them, they persisted in burning the palm fronds, as they had always done.

Mosquitoes plagued the atolls and transmitted dengue fever, which could be fatal for young children. On Poro Poro, Bernard poured a few drops of kerosene on the surface of the water that lay in ruts and in the holes dug by sand crabs. The mosquitoes disappeared from the motu. He explained his method to the villagers. Only Neti and Raumati used the technique.

Neti was the disciple Bernard had converted to his ideas. He was his best friend on the atoll: "Twin brothers united by the same thoughts." He reminded him of Xaï, his alter ego in the village of the Gulf of Siam. Together they went hunting on the outer reef and gathered copra on the motus that surround the lagoon.

Bernard was troubled by the great damage caused by rats eating the coconuts and tried to find a remedy. One solution was to protect the coconuts from the attacks by ringing the tree trunks with metal sheets that came from the printing press of *La Dépêche de Tahiti*. Papeete had sent some to the atolls and Bernard had discovered a whole cache lying forgotten amongst the junk behind Neti's house. He used the technique successfully on the Poro Poro palms and was able to drink the milk of his coconuts. But ringing the trees was hard work, and too much trouble for the Paumotus.

Two mornings a week, Moitessier went on board JOSHUA, painted, sewed the mizzen, did odds and ends, and wrote. He sailed to Suvorov for the third time with Iléana and Stephan. They found Tom who, even at 74, was still at work feeding his 40 chickens and tending his kitchen garden.

"Tom is a fountain of youth," said Bernard. On Bird Island they had the pleasure of drinking milk from the coconuts planted five years earlier, and on the way back, they lazed for a while in Bora Bora before returning to Tahiti and then Ahé.

The cruise to Suvorov and the example set by Tom gave them the necessary stimulus for the big project they were working on, which was to improve the coconut harvest and copra production by eliminating the rats. While having lunch at Dominique Charnay's, Bernard outlined his strategy to Antoine, a popular French singer. *"A rat eats five coconuts per month, that's two pounds of copra, or 24 pounds of copra per year. If ten cats eat three thousand rats in one year, they will have saved 36 tons of copra."*[4]

It was brilliantly clear to Bernard that he'd found the solution: All he had to do was bring cats to Ahé. A dozen of them would give birth to kittens, and their multiplying would mean the end of the rats.

Neti met Bernard in Papeete. An excellent sailor like all Paumotus, he helped Bernard sail back to Ahé. They gathered up 18 kittens in Tahiti and brought them aboard JOSHUA. The voyage to bring them back was epic because the kittens were constantly escaping from their cardboard boxes. A few other kittens brought in by Iléana on the island schooner or sent from a neighboring island completed the anti-rat brigade.

The cats were distributed among the families on the island.

The villagers were assembled and Bernard explained to them patiently what he had in mind: the cats would hunt the rats, and the production of copra would increase, bringing prosperity to the atoll. Tepuku understood what was at stake. *"All those young people who went to look for work in Tahiti will come back."* Raumati looked farther ahead: *"When they come back to the island, there will be enough people to replace the old coconut trees."*[5] The stakes were enormous: All of the Tuamotus could benefit.

Bernard and Iléana returned from a four-month absence, happy to be back among their plantings. The papayas were heavy with fruit and the ringed coconut palms had grown. The garden, on the other hand, needed care, and they had to treat the water again to kill the mosquito larvae. Four weeks later, when they got around to inquiring about the war against the rats, they were appalled. Most of the families had let the kittens in their charge die of hunger. Iléana was so upset she even talked of leaving Polynesia. "I was hoping people would have understood faster," said Bernard, saddened.

In his long letter of June 17, 1978 to Jean Knocker, Moitessier described another experience.

I had organized a group of fourteen courageous workers, including myself. The aim was to create new coconut groves on virgin land. The work consisted in clearing the brush. Then the rainy season would come and every one would plant at that time. The fourteen guys of the group worked fourteen times, two days a week. Then Iléana and I went back to Tahiti, and returned six months later. The rainy season had been exceptional; everything was green. But not one coconut tree had been planted on the cleared land.

The Paumotus had forgotten why they had performed this enormous amount of work.

In January 1978, Moitessier took on a cargo of fruit trees in Tahiti. He loaded 60 standing mango and avocado trees and also a stem of bananas and a carton of mangoes and grapefruit for the children of Ahé. Dominique Charnay went along. For three days Bernard sailed as he was accustomed to, in reflection and silence, which unsettled Charnay. When Charnay mentioned this, Bernard explained: "Sailing is like a religion. You have to listen to your boat." Then he talked about Indochina where, as Stephan was doing in Ahé, he had acquired "the intelligence of the body."

The trees were given to Arri, the young mayor of Ahé, who had the task of distributing them among the villagers. To Bernard's surprise, a "day of the trees" was organized. The village became a work zone: The men dug, moved good soil they'd found in one of the motus, chopped up trunks of banana trees to create humus, and planted an avocado or mango tree in front of each faré. Bernard cried out: "They understand the earth!"

⁂

Bernard and Iléana were contented. At peace with themselves, they tended their garden, harvesting bok choy, watermelons, and cucumbers. Bernard swam, dove for fish, and learned how to use a *patia*, a Polynesian spear like a trident used for harpooning fish. To use it efficiently you have to account for the refraction of the water. Stephan was thriving. He went to school in the mornings and began to read Chinese characters. He paddled in the shallows and played with his friends in the village, where the older children kept an eye on the younger ones. He became skilful with a slingshot and screamed with delight when he speared his first mullet with the small patia his father made for him. Bernard was happy. *"It certainly was the first time I felt so totally at peace with myself. It was a long-term peace, without any crazy projects in mind, without my hatching some big plan to save the world."*[6]

Gaston Floss, counselor to the Territorial Assembly and future president of French Polynesia, visited Ahé while campaigning. Bernard, sitting in a yoga position on a large steel drum, listened as he expounded his theories on the future of the territories and the prosperity that would come from the harvesting, as yet theoretical, of metallic nodules. Charnay, who was present at the meeting, related Moitessier's response.

> It is a question of choice. The budget represents only physical energy. The human being represents mental energy. The budget can be compared to a bulldozer. The human being with his conscience, his choice, is on the bulldozer. And depending on the choice man makes, the bulldozer can lay bare the mountain and destroy it, or he can replant the mountain and create a world.

Despite the serenity he'd found there, after 18 months on Ahé, Bernard was fully aware that while he'd been enriched by the experience it had its limitations. He didn't kid himself. Growing vegetables and fruit on a coral reef required enormous and constant effort. He knew also that the Paumotus were not going to change their habits. They would continue to burn the palm fronds, eat imported rice with the fish they caught in the lagoon, open cans of corned beef, and let the rats ruin the coconut groves.

The Polynesia's lure is the notion of easy living without a care for the future, symbolized by the expression *aieta pea pea* "it doesn't matter." But the pleasure of existing from one day to the next in a dream setting and an ideal climate, in idleness punctuated by the occasional spell of hard work, made it impossible to have any long-term plan. In Fatu Hiva, which we visited four times between 1975 and 1999, we witnessed the erosion of traditional ways. This island in the Marquesas has been blessed by the gods with an abundance of coffee, grapefruit, mango, and orange trees and in the mountains, cattle, pigs, and goats living wild, there for the hunting. But the Marquesans prefer instant coffee, canned fruit, condensed milk, and canned meat. When we expressed surprise at their expensive habits and asked why they didn't use what was available fresh, they simply smiled and said, "Too much work."

Moitessier decided to leave Ahé, to put an end to this utopia of foolish generosity and his dream to teach the Paumotus to use their ecology. He loved the atoll deeply, had enjoyed Neti's friendship, and admired Raumati's skill with the patia and Tuare's talent at spearfishing. He promised, "I'll come back." But Tepuku and Raumati were moving to the next atoll and Neti went to work as mate on a copra schooner.

In 1982, we stopped in Ahé. On Poro Poro, Tepuku was

repairing the roof of Bernard's faré, convinced that he would soon come back to the serenity of his lagoon.

But the seeker of truth had turned the page. As if the Dragon, asleep for a while, had stirred. A new idea to save the world had germinated in Moitessier's brain.

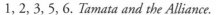

1, 2, 3, 5, 6. *Tamata and the Alliance.*
4. *Moitessier, le chemin des îles.*

17

The fruit trees

After leaving Ahé, Bernard and Iléana moved to Moorea. An hour away from Tahiti by boat, this smaller, quieter island with its steep-sloped mountains, its lagoon, and its two deep, well-protected bays, has a primitive beauty. Iléana had found an old ramshackle faré with a garden where Bernard, who needed physical activity and intimate contact with the soil, could grow vegetables. Luckily the rent was minimal, since over time the royalties had declined considerably. Moitessier wrote a somewhat wry letter to Uncle Jean.

> The faré is a ruin, but this is exactly the kind of accommodation Iléana and I like. At any rate the roof doesn't leak much and I took care of the drafts with a few nails

and a bit of plywood. As for the leaks in the roof, it's very easy: we put a can under each leak. The can fills up when it rains a lot and the water evaporates when it's warm, a sort of variation on perpetual motion.

Iléana again took up sewing the pareus that sold so well in the tourist shops. Stephan went back to school. Bernard was happy to be among friends with whom he could discuss the future of the world. He disclosed to Jean Knocker that he wanted to write a technical book and intended to concentrate on it in his new surroundings in Moorea.

Moitessier had always been interested in trying to find ways to sail well on limited means. From Ahé, he had written a five-page letter to JOSHUA's builder, Fricaud, warning him against the various innovations he had in mind, such as hulls of heavy steel plates with built-in anodes, and centerboards. "Jo is charming, brilliant in his specialty and I like him a lot. But at the same time I'm very wary of how quickly he jumps on the ideas going through his head."

Bernard filled pages and pages of an exercise book with notes and sketches. At the same time, he was thinking of another book, the book he'd been carrying inside him since Indochina. In the easy living in Polynesia he found it difficult to start writing. However, he had a role model nearby. Along Moorea's lagoon lived a writer, Jean-Marie Dallet, his wife Michèle, a talented painter, and their neighbor, Christian Jonville, a doctor and a sailor.

Dallet was writing a fictionalized biography of Gauguin, whom both he and Bernard admired. The sailor, hungry for intellectual discussions, visited the writer quite often and borrowed books from him. "He often came unexpectedly," Dallet remembered, "and would sit in the lotus position and expound big utopian theories containing some grains of common-sense . . . Self-taught, he was discovering things by experience, late in life. Including philosophy: he was learning by himself things that were already well established and he adopted some of those ideas with an endearing freshness and spontaneity."

He interrupted the monotony of his simple and routine existence—"almost two years of contemplating the passing of the days in the joy of living"—with a fourth trip to Suvorov, this time solo. But old Tom was no longer there. At 75, suffering from cancer, he had been taken to the hospital in Rarotonga, where he died. All that remained of him on his atoll were the vestiges of his incredible efforts and the guidelines he'd left for visitors on how to take care of Anchorage Island. Passing sailors wrote down in a notebook what they had accomplished—fixing up the faré, painting, clearing the brush, feeding the chickens—and made suggestions as to what needed to be done next.

⁕

As he often did, after a period of inaction, Moitessier felt a great need for activity. He wanted to accomplish what he called "a big project." He started thinking about it in Ahé, on board JOSHUA. Twice a week, he went on board to do a little work, paint, write or, sitting at the chart table, simply dream. He wanted to keep up the relationship with the boat that had taken him on the long way. Sometimes he stayed overnight.

A memory persisted from his childhood in Indochina. Lining his route to school were mango trees offering their fruit to passers by. With Stephan, he himself had planted fruit trees along the roads near their faré in Tahiti. Why not bring this practice to the villages and towns of France? A conversation he had in 1974 on the train to Le Croisic to visit Le Toumelin had revived that idea. *"By planting fruit trees everywhere we would accomplish together something generous and simple at the same time, something that would show a change in our mindsets."*[1]

In 1976, he had sent a check for 15,000 francs ($3,000) to his friend Alain Hervé, asking him to find a town hall that would use the money to plant fruit trees in the community. He'd made the same suggestion to a high official he knew. The official was critical of the project: the children would get diarrhea from eating the unripe fruits and besides they might get stung by wasps. This reaction, which Bernard thought idiotic, hadn't discouraged him. On board his boat one night, he wrote several drafts of a letter to send to mayors. It had remained forgotten in a drawer on the ketch and, in the absence of a candidate, Alain Hervé had returned the check. Four years later, he came back to the same idea, with a vengeance. In March and April 1980 he sent a slew of letters all over the world.

March 4, 1980

To His Excellency the Ambassador of the Republic of China

Fruit trees planted along the roads and paths, in the cities' streets and in the forests, would hurt neither man's nor the country's soul. These fruit trees would probably bring a moral and physical aid to the people of countries who realized in time this moment of evolution, of creation.

He mentioned as an example the mango trees he and Iléana had planted next to a parking lot and that now bore fruit which children ate and provided shade under which it was pleasant to have a chat.

The French mayors, through their association newsletter, the media, artists including Antoine, Brigitte Bardot, Jean Ferrat, Alain Souchon, Guy Béart, Georges Brassens, and others, received a similar message.

Here is an idea that I think is a good one, even though it came to me in a dream: to plant fruit trees along all our roads and paths . . . A fruit tree gives both the shade and greenery we need, as well as fruit.

Fruit trees that belonged to everyone without being anyone's private property would stand as a symbol of the era of change we have to embark on. As they grow, those fruit trees could become real, silent participants in creating something bigger than our small selves, a work both generous and simple which would help to unite people on the path to the evolution of intelligence.

Some newspapers responded negatively. Moitessier had an unfriendly exchange with *L'Express.*

March 18, 1980

Unfortunately our weekly does not have enough space to publish all the proposals or requests we are inundated with daily.

Jean-François Revel

Moitessier was irate, probably unjustly.

April 28, 1980

If the world comes to an end one day, it will be because of stupidity. When the senior editor of a magazine with a circulation of half a million copies all over France and overseas seems more interested in the distant past of Marchais [a French communist politician] than in much more essential problems relevant to creation . . . then in my opinion the editor of that magazine sins by stupidity and omission.

Other newspapers were more open to the idea. Stories appeared in *Le Monde, Le Figaro, Le Nouvel Observateur,* Alain Hervé's *Le Sauvage,* and nautical magazines. Dominique Charnay, who had left Tahiti and was now a journalist in Paris, published an article in a nautical magazine. Television and radio programs mentioned the sailor's proposal. He added a promise to his request. He would give 15,000 francs to the first mayor who would respond positively. The first application came from Georges Lambert, the mayor of Lachelle, by telegram. He later wrote:

April 24, 1980

Since 1971, when my Municipal Council was elected, we have wanted to add to the attraction of a rural community by planting fruit trees along the various village roads, but financial difficulties did not allow us to do so.

Lachelle is a village of 317 inhabitants, near Compiègne in the northeast of France, surrounded by fields of beets. It has one of the highest agricultural yields in France. A hedge had already been planted with cherry trees, each bearing the name of a child of the community. On April 30, the check for 15,000 francs was sent to Georges Lambert, the jolly local councilor, himself a farmer. Answering to *Le Figaro* over the phone, Moitessier explained: "Knowing that you can participate yourself in the cycle of life awakens many things in a person's conscience."

He admitted that he wasn't rich: the money sent to Lachelle, and the sums he allocated to other municipalities that answered his call depleted his meager resources. He had no regrets. *"You cannot be wrong when you participate in generous causes."*[2]

Sixty-two other municipalities answered and Moitessier took the trouble to write back to all of them. In Calvados, Normandy, a thruway rest area was planted with apple trees. In Alsace, a letter writer said, "I have always seen apple, pear, and cherry trees along the roads, and the townsfolk on their Sunday stroll would pick up the ripe fruit that had fallen on the ground."

The fruit trees

On his return to France, Bernard went to Lachelle to view the plantings of apple, cherry, and nut trees—hundreds of hazel trees on a knoll of about an acre. On December 10, 1996, with a group of the sailor's friends in attendance, 260 more trees were planted. On March 22, 2003, the project was reopened, with each child of the village in charge of a tree, to replace the ailing apple trees and plant mulberry trees.

Under the aegis of Georges Lambert, Lachelle has become a symbol for ecological awareness. Among its street names are Peace Street, Street of the Apple Trees, Street of the Hazel Trees, and its swimming pool is heated by solar panels. The village preserves the memory of the sailor with Bernard Moitessier Street and a fresco with a maritime theme created by the children of the elementary school.

Lachelle's example didn't find much of a following in other villages or towns. Once again, even if he wasn't sorry for having tried, Bernard had to admit that he was naïve and that, however noble the motive, it was very difficult to get people out of their routine and inertia.

<hr />

1. Diary of Bernard Moitessier.
2. Le Figaro, June 5, 1980.

18

The United States

In a letter dated April 28, 1980, Bernard announced:

> Next project: leave solo in a month for Hawaii and California. I need to go to sea, breathe the sea air and see other faces, recharge my batteries running somewhat on empty after eleven years in a country that made little mental or creative demands. Iléana and Stephan will come later.

He was more explicit in a letter to Jean Knocker:

> June 14, 1980
>
> We are in Tahiti, absolutely fed-up (for the time being) with Polynesia. I am getting ready to sail to San Fran-

cisco, departing early August. I won't stop in Hawaii because it will be late for the season.

The decision to leave for the United States, to find renewed energy for writing the book he had not yet started and give Stephan new surroundings more suited to his needs, stemmed from an encounter during his third stop in Suvorov. Aboard PHOBOS, a large American ketch anchored there, were a couple and their child. Maurice was a year older than Stephan, and the two little boys quickly became pals. Ugo and Isabella invited the French sailors for dinner.

Ugo, a research engineer at Berkeley, was an excellent underwater spear fisherman. Through his quiet strength he exerted a strong influence on Moitessier and became one of his most important mentors. Ugo and Isabella decided to stay longer. *"At each sunrise—like Stephan and Maurice, and like Isabella and Iléana—Ugo and I felt the urgency to imbue each other with the best part of ourselves."*[1]

When Bernard complained that he was tired of Polynesia, Iléana made a suggestion. *"At Suvorov, Ugo and Isabella often talked about California. From north to south the whole coast is dotted with yacht clubs—and you're famous there. You have the movie you shot during the long way and its images are just breathtaking. With you there to introduce it at screenings, you'll pack the halls. The United States will be the final key which will at last open the door to your writing."*[2]

Bernard knew how clear sighted Iléana could be. It was she who'd convinced him in the end to renounce his royalties, who'd suggested her despondent companion visit Phil in Israel.

She discovered Ahé, and found the faré in Moorea. Once again, she was the one making the decision. First, she said, JOSHUA had to be put back in shape.

During the two years of idleness, the ketch had received hardly any care. In Tahiti, the smallest job cost a fortune and, in accordance with the prevailing attitude *aita pea-pea* (it doesn't matter), took forever. Luck always seemed to favor Moitessier when he most needed it; this time it came by the name of KIM, a 38-foot steel ketch. The four young men who had designed and built this boat were planning to go from Polynesia to Tierra del Fuego and Antarctica.

The amount of work needed on JOSHUA didn't faze them. "If you can arrange to get your boat hauled out at the navy shipyard, we can knock off the work in a week. For free, of course." Another miracle followed. A phone call from a friend to the dockyard chief settled the matter. "The hoist will take you tomorrow morning at eight o'clock sharp. You'll be put back in the water ten days later, at the latest." All of this at no cost. Bernard wrote to me.

April 28, 1980

They helped me tremendously to get JOSHUA back into shape. Thanks to them I now have a brand new boat (everything on deck has been redone: hand rails, stanchions, bitts, pulpits and pushpits, cleats, fiferails, even the bowsprit). Not to mention a few little things welded out of stainless to replace plain steel that rusts badly. To make a long story short, I really have a boat not only new but finished—18 years after it was first launched—which proves that I was right to start sailing right away 18 years ago and not wait until I finished the boat at the end of 1979.

The ketch was ready and the season was right since summer is the best time to arrive in California. What was he waiting for? He explained it to me.

May 24, 1980

This business with the trees took a lot of my time. The moment will come when I'll have to concentrate exclusively on getting ready. As you know, I have to prepare psychologically, too, not just technically. You have to have left already in your mind before doing it physically. You know this as well as I do. It's a serious matter and it's through forgetting this or not recognizing it that a number of passages ended up in accidents or total disaster.

Just then, a windsurfing extremist, Arnaud de Rosnay, arrived in Polynesia. Good-looking in a playboy kind of way, this adventurer, having crossed the Bering Strait on a windsurfer, was ready to tackle the Pacific Ocean. Bernard had long conversations with him at the home of Mico Sauzier, a friend from the Mauritius days and a cousin of Arnaud. The windsurfer fascinated Bernard, "one of those rare guys a god on Olympus could fall in love with." But he wasn't a sailor. In a series of letters, which were interesting because they showed how he looked out for others, Moitessier expressed both his admiration and his doubts.

August 11, 1980

Met yesterday Arnaud de Rosnay who will windsurf from the Marquesas to Hawaii . . . This is a big project. I hope he will succeed. Cameramen shot miles of film and pestered us to death during the five or six hours I spent with Rosnay showing him how to use a sextant (he's very talented) and calculate latitude. I copied the sun's declinations for him onto one page, from August 22 to October 23. He's going to laminate it and it might save his life if he loses contact with the support boat.

Bernard gave me the detailed solutions Arnaud had arrived at for making distilled water and feeding himself—with NASA pills—and described the board "made so you can sleep on it, and keep warm, protected from the wind and the spray." He said he trusted the man's abilities, and he was amazed by "the incredible host of photographers, American TV, and hangers on who followed him around." But his doubts mounted when he found out that the windsurfer hadn't tested the equipment on a passage that entailed a night at sea. "I think he needs at least some divine help to try such an adventure." Ever generous, Moitessier wanted to help Rosnay.

August 14

Had dinner the day before yesterday at Mico's with Arnaud. We organized this meeting, just the two of us, away from the media, to be able to discuss seriously and in depth the essentials of survival, the safest route, and the sea.

With the help of a sketch, Bernard explained to me how Rosnay's board could be transformed into a trimaran by placing the mast across it with inflatable tubes attached at both ends. Arnaud was to be escorted, first by the French Navy, then by ZEUS, a 40-foot sailboat belonging to an excellent sailor whom Moitessier made a point of meeting. The hardest part was to not lose contact, which both sailors agreed had a 90-percent likelihood of happening. Bernard was worried. Once the windsurfer was alone, what would happen if the mast broke? There was always the kite:

I tried to get him to make a strong point on the bow of his board with a block for the kite line. And if he loses the kite after losing the mast? Well, he doesn't even have a paddle. I discussed all of this with him. But he didn't listen. I explained to him that with a small 28-inch underwater gun + a paddle + a sextant + a solar still, he could manage come what may. His answer was, "This is out of the question, it's far too dangerous and could puncture the inflatable tubes." I gave him my diving goggles. He'll probably forget them.

Despite everything I told you, and what I felt, what I saw and understood, I still think he has a 99% chance to reach Hawaii. Some guys are beloved by the gods.

The next day, he wrote again at length about Arnaud's adventure.

August 15, 1980

All I wrote to you yesterday concerning my doubts and worries about Arnaud's technical knowledge and the weakness of his equipment is all baloney . . . and a lesson in wisdom and humility for me.

The hero of *the long way* spent five hours alone with Arnaud. Together they boarded the windsurfer set up in its trimaran mode. Bernard checked out its buoyancy, stability, and comfort and went over the practicalities of navigation and survival after losing contact with the support boat. "It is absolutely perfect," he said, adding "I thought of leaving tomorrow Saturday. But the wind's blowing like crazy. I'll wait until things quiet down."

Before leaving, he wrote a last message to Arnaud that was pure Moitessier.

August 17

To conquer the Dragon, you will have to defeat him three times.

The first time will be in the first 700 miles, where the struggle will arise between the true Arnaud and the false Arnaud. After you win this first battle, the Dragon will come out of his lair. Taking advantage of your fatigue, he will dazzle you with all manner of enticements physical and psychological to lure you into the trap of the direct course, which isn't a good course.

When you emerge victorious from this second battle, the Dragon will await you to the east of your goal and will try using your elation to get you mesmerized by a latitude too good to be true.

You will defeat the Dragon, if you have taken to heart the lesson of the first two battles to unify your body, your spirit, and your soul and to stay alert in all circumstances. You will pay attention to the current, which runs southward in this season in the approaches to Hawaii; you will pay attention to everything during this third and final encounter between the two Arnauds. Many friends will be looking out for you and will try to help you but you alone can win your fearsome battle and defeat the Dragon.

As it turned out, several of Bernard's recommendations proved useless because the Polynesian authorities didn't let Rosnay go through with his project. He made instead a much shorter passage of 500 miles. Leaving the Marquesas on August 31 heading southeast, he reached Ahé 12 days later at an average speed of about two knots. It was so slow, in spite of the favorable winds and current, that the observers became worried. Bernard had left Tahiti on August 25 and it was Iléana who wrote about the happy outcome of the windsurfer's adventure, "I always hoped he would find an island on his way. Bernard instinctively realized Arnaud's potential. Something indefinable happened that reassured him."

JOSHUA's passage from Tahiti to California, of nearly 5,000 miles, was favored with a southeast wind that persisted even north of the Equator, and then a southwesterly wind on the approach to San Francisco. The threat of a hurricane had Bernard worried. He'd just caught a large dorado and he threw it back in the sea, begging it to ask the storm to go and blow somewhere else. The fish obliged. His only problem was the sails. While the mainsail was new and the mizzen was in good shape, the others were dying one after another. A staysail and a storm jib dating from *the long way* were the last ones left. JOSHUA arrived in California early October, after 38 days at sea, and anchored in Sausalito, in San Francisco Bay. Iléana and Stephan joined him. A new life was beginning for them. Bernard wrote to me, "Since my arrival, I've been overwhelmed by the change of pace."

He was in urgent need of money. The marina had to be paid, $270 a month, then there was Stephan's tuition and the telephone on board. He could no longer go barefoot in old shorts and a straw hat. Isabella, his friend from Suvorov, took him to a second-hand-clothing store. For $20 he bought a pair of corduroys, two shirts, a down vest, a good pair of shoes, and two pairs of wool socks. With the help of the owner of a charter company, he wrote and printed a four-page, full color brochure in which he gave his biography, described his 10-month solo circumnavigation, and reiterated his call for planting fruit trees. He offered talks and film screenings to the local yacht clubs and tried to get the English version of *The Long Way* reprinted.

The United States seemed to have brought him renewed energy and optimism.

November 5, 1980

With the help of a competent friend, I fixed the film of *The Long Way.* It now runs for forty-two minutes. All the uninteresting sequences have been cut and the chronology reestablished. First showing on January 9 ($250) and another in April-May ($500).

I'm looking for a public relations person to organize a tour of screenings/seminars. Also I got in contact with Phil Thurmann at *Pacific Skipper.* I'm going to write an article a month for the magazine; that should help to keep food on the table.

Here's the opinion of the friend who helped me with the movie (Italian born, naturalized American): an American will think of you as a friend until proven the contrary, while a Mediterranean will see you as an enemy until proven different.

My brochure will be redone professionally with big headlines and blurbs. On the back, I will offer the following: learn how to use a sextant + latitude + longitude by HO249 sun + stars in one day (your money back if you don't get it).

Six months later, the system was working. Bernard had found an agent to negotiate his fees, and he was giving his twenty-first talk. The film impressed his audiences and they also listened with interest to his pitch about the fruit trees. The San Francisco Maritime Institute asked him to do a seminar for future circumnavigators, in groups of eight or 10, for which Moitessier was paid $125 per participant.

But in October 1981, a year after JOSHUA's arrival in the United States, the situation was totally different. In order to renew their visas, they had to go abroad. Canada and Mexico were the closest, but going to either country on JOSHUA presented problems. Heading north they would meet with heavy weather, mists, and vicious currents, and to the south it was hurricane season. Besides, the ketch wasn't ready for such a voyage. The bottom needed scrubbing and she didn't have the right foresails.

Bernard and Iléana got in touch with an expensive specialist lawyer. They ended up traveling to Vancouver and back. Getting their visas took the last of their money. A letter of October 16, 1981 put me in the picture.

A lot of downs and practically no ups since my last letter. Work is very hard. The government clamped down on the budget for education; as a result the universities and other schools ignore my brochure. I was left with my secret weapon: cruising lessons for people who come to spend a day with me one on one aboard JOSHUA. I advertised in *SAIL, Cruising World,* and *Latitude 38* (the ads cost me almost $600) but I'm far from recuperating that money; it's almost complete failure.

Not everything was negative for Bernard. A dentist redid most of his teeth in exchange for a sailing course on board his boat. But his ulcer erupted again, and he had to be hospitalized and have a blood transfusion. He refused to be operated on. Iléana was selling hardly any of the dresses she designed and sewed. They were nearly destitute. By November he recognized that he was in survival mode.

By chance, after a screening, a building contractor in the audience offered him a job working two or three days a week for $10 an hour. Bernard dug holes, pushed a wheelbarrow, and mixed cement. Gamely, he said, "It's excellent for me to break out in a sweat once in a while."

The family found a home. A couple offered them a cottage on their property, 40 miles from San Francisco, with a swimming pool, a car, and $500 a month in exchange for gardening and 10 hours work a week from Bernard, five hours from Iléana. Moitessier was full of hope.

November 28, 1981

I feel I am out of the hole, that things will sort themselves out.

⸺⟨∞⟩⸺

1, 2. *Tamata and the Alliance.*

19

The loss of JOSHUA

The American dream was coming to naught. Moitessier shared his disappointment with me.

> I had come to this country to make a bit of money and push my ideas at the same time (with the movie + the story of the fruit trees) so I could retire into a corner and write that book we'd talked about . . . I gave about thirty talks, each time mentioning the fruit trees; people seemed truly interested but at the same time I had the feeling they couldn't care less. I've lost most of my illusions about the United States. The dollar is in practically every conversation.

He didn't make any real friends, except for Ugo and Isabella, who were both of Italian origin. He wanted to leave. After Ahé, Polynesia, and Suvorov, this universe of asphalt, concrete, and highways and its sterile crowds made him nostalgic for the soil. He wanted to flee, but he was trapped. A French organization, "Galas de la Mer," invited him to show his movie. *Neptune nautisme* would pay for his flight in exchange for an article. He politely turned them down. "I went through a hard time and I'm starting from scratch. Besides the fact that a quick trip to the Boat Show would be exhausting, I also have other engagements here that I cannot postpone without wasting months of preparation."

Bernard and Iléana quit their caretaking job and had to leave the house that came with it. Doing maintenance work after a full day's work on the construction site left Moitessier without any energy. He just wanted to sleep. It took him an hour and a half to two hours on the highway to get to the job site, and then there was the cost of gas and all the other expenses. They had to go back to living on the boat in order to resume maintenance in readiness for the students he was expecting on his navigation course. The monthly marina fee of $270, Stephan's school tuition, and the cost of health insurance and food were together reducing them to poverty. "I understood that my life in this country would consist of working like a nut just to make ends meet and no more." It was time to go somewhere else. But where? He explored that question in the letter he sent me.

Asia is out. The Pacific? We've tried it. Of course it's better than starving and freezing in France or the U.S. Africa? Start all over again, at almost 60, with no money, in areas where white people are not exactly welcome. South America? No idea, we know nothing about it.

He was 57. He had grown thin, he was tired, and he had to admit that he no longer had the energy that had allowed him to start all over again each time fate had dealt him a blow.

He needed to leave, but not right away. "We don't even have a choice if we want to head for fairer skies. No money (none whatsoever), no provisions, no genoa or jib and the stay-sail is in such bad shape that I can't sew it together any more, I can only patch it." Finally, he decided to get under way, even with a boat in such bad condition. He was thinking of Costa Rica, where things were cheap, or of going back to Polynesia. And, as happened time and again in Bernard's life, providence intervened at a crucial moment.

When a local paper announced his imminent departure, customers flocked to enroll in his navigation courses. In three months, the kitty was flush. And, just before they left for Europe on vacation, Ugo and Isabella asked him for the dimensions of JOSHUA's sails. Three weeks later, the boat received a miraculous present: two jibs, a staysail, and a genoa, custom made in Italy.

Another encounter helped the sailor with his plans. Klaus Kinski, the actor, dreamed of sailing around the world. He wrote in a book, "Chichester, Chay Blyth, Tabarly, Moitessier are becoming my heroes." He quite often visited the Sausalito marina and suddenly decided he wanted to go to Tahiti aboard JOSHUA. He offered $30,000. It was a gift from heaven. However his complex personality worried Bernard. "A friend told me that he is half crazy, totally unpredictable, that he attracts disaster." In the end, because he had to shoot a movie, Kinski could only go for two weeks, as far as Mexico. The agreed price was $5,000. This was still a decent offer.

Iléana and Stephan would stay in the U.S. Stephan was happy in school and was steadily perfecting his English. Iléana didn't want to return to the intellectual desert of the tropics. "She has a chance to learn something interesting, something artistic, and also something about both medicinal and wild edible plants," Bernard wrote Jean Knocker when he announced that they were separating, at least for the time being.

He wrote in *Tamata and the Alliance*, "Iléana and I already knew that separation had become inevitable, and probably final. She knew she would always be in my heart, whatever happened." Then why? Because, he said, "the gods so willed it." Even if the solo sailor had warned his companion from the beginning that he planned to keep his freedom, some would take exception to this explanation and find it somewhat cavalier, especially when Iléana had helped Bernard many times in difficult circumstances with her unselfish advice.

On November 21, 1982 JOSHUA sailed from San Francisco Bay with Bernard Moitessier and Klaus Kinski on board. The boat carried stores and supplies enough to last for a long time. Three weeks later I received a letter from Iléana and Stephan.

Tuesday, December 14, 1982

I am writing with very sad news because I don't think Bernard has the heart to let you know. JOSHUA has become a wreck full of water and sand.

What happened? Moitessier had an article published in *Cruising World* relating the story and in which he also praised his crew, "a marvelous, simple, warm, and interesting person." The voyage started in a light breeze, then a southeasterly gale, after which they had fine following winds. On Friday, December 3, after 12 days, the ketch anchored in the Bay of Cabo San Lucas. Dominique Charnay gave a totally different version of Bernard's description of his part-time crew. He was unskilled and he was particularly inept at handling the dinghy. His constant capsizes when approaching the beach had become a spectator sport. It was for this reason that Bernard anchored in the middle of the flotilla of boats, as close as possible to shore.

Kinski still had another few days and Bernard tried to teach him celestial navigation. Despite Bernard's teaching skills, the actor seemed allergic to math. On December 8, at about 5 p.m., Klaus had finally acquired the basics of celestial navigation. He had familiarized himself with the sextant during the course of the passage. A taxi was picking him up the next day to take him to the airport.

Cabo San Lucas, the first stop on the Mexican coast, is well known for its clear waters and is a favorite place for cruisers in the winter season. The hurricane season had been over for two months. The records were unanimous: No hurricane ever came after October. The anchorage was well protected except from easterly winds, which only blow in the bad season.

On December 8, at around noon, the sky became overcast with clouds moving in rapidly from the southeast. It started raining and the wind blew hard for half an hour. A swell began to build. As a precaution, Moitessier prepared a second anchor, a 45-pound CQR, with 100 feet of chain and 300 feet of line coiled on deck. At dusk the wind started blowing from the southeast, "not too strongly, but I didn't like it," Bernard said, adding, "I knew (I think I knew) it couldn't last in this season."

The wind strengthened during the night and 10-foot waves were breaking on the beach. Moitessier was on deck. Suddenly the 55-pound CQR dragged. He dropped the second anchor. The swell grew bigger yet. In a strong gust that seemed endless, the second anchor dragged. Some boats tried to get under way but their propellers got caught in the anchor rodes, adding to the confusion. JOSHUA was driven toward the beach. The rudder struck first, then the boat pivoted around and lay beam on to the breaking waves. Bernard and Klaus started arguing.

"Klaus, take your things and jump right now."

"I won't leave you alone. I'm staying with you, you'll need help."

Bernard insisted, got mad. "He could not understand that I had to stay on my boat, that this was what I had to do. I couldn't leave my boat and take off like that."

To persuade Kinski to go on land before it was too late, before the waves became lethal, Moitessier explained to him that he had been through two shipwrecks, that he had been sailing on JOSHUA for 21 years, and that, danger or not, he had to stay on board. Kinski left. An hour and a half later, it would have been impossible to land. Bernard sat down on the cabin sole and thought.

> I can now see clearly the signs that my brain ignored, the signs in the sky and the clouds coming from offshore. I was teaching Klaus the stars and the sea but I was look-ing at the sky with the eyes of a blind man. Besides I was anchored too close to the beach, too close to other boats, and left myself no possibility for maneuvering when there was still time to head for the open sea.

Another yacht rammed the ketch, taking out her rig and pushing both of them deeper into the sand.

By dawn the beach had become a cemetery. Twenty-six wrecks lay on the sand like dead fish; two other boats had sunk, luckily without loss of life.

JOSHUA was strong enough to have survived, but the masts were broken, the stanchions and pulpits flattened, hatches shattered, and the cabin doors ripped off. The rudder was gone and the hull was full of sand and water in which floated mattresses, cushions, bottles, sails; books and notebooks had turned to pulp.

A very generous couple, Bill and Laura, opened their door to Bernard and a couple of shipwrecked sailors. Ugo hopped on the first plane to come to his aid. Two young men, a Swiss and an American, helped Bernard retrieve some gear: anchors, chains, tools, sails, compass, and sextant which Bill and Laura let him store in their garage. But the precious notes for the future book were lost.

JOSHUA could not be left to die. A crew spent a week to dig a trench. Reto Filli, who had come to help, offered to buy the boat, though he didn't have much money. Bernard gave her to him; what money Reto had, he would use to put the boat back in shape.

On the day of the new moon, at high tide, a bulldozer freed JOSHUA from the wrecked FREILING. On board, ten volunteers worked desperately to remove the sand and water. The Caterpillar pushed and the keel slid over the sand and reached the water. Bernard and two helpers heaved on the warp of the anchor he'd set offshore. The boat was then secured with three anchors. The hull was battered, but it didn't leak a drop.

—∞∞—

Bernard was asked the same question many times. "If you had to do it all over again, would you build the same boat?" His answer was unequivocal.

> When I built JOSHUA, I was 37. The ketch was perfect for the life I wanted to lead. With the passing of time, I have to admit that JOSHUA needs more maintenance than I can provide. At sea, that was no problem, but for the rest of the time, it has become bigger than I need. If I had to have another boat, it would be a steel boat too but much smaller and with a transom.

In a letter sent from Cabo San Lucas on January 7, 1983, Bernard told me he was in good shape mentally. "JOSHUA was the perfect boat for my lifestyle until the last few years. Then my life changed. In a way, this setback was for the best, and the fact that JOSHUA is in the hands of a young man who will take care of her is a good thing."

It was impossible to imagine Bernard without a boat. As they had after the shipwrecks of MARIE-THÉRÈSE and MARIE-THÉRÈSE II, his guardian angels came to the rescue. Rick Wood, an American sailor who had rounded Cape Horn on a steel ketch and whom Bernard had met in Tahiti, had set up a boatyard in San Francisco Bay. As luck would have it, John Hutton and his companion, Ned, who had also been in the same anchorage in Tahiti with JOSHUA and had become friends with Bernard, had just finished building a steel boat in Rick's yard. Two days after Ugo returned to San Francisco, John called Bernard. "We're not going to let you down. Ned and I will build a new boat for you." Ugo wrote a check for $3,000, the cost of the steel. Rick confirmed the deal, "I can have the steel delivered tomorrow afternoon. John and Ned can use all our tools. And I won't ask you for a cent. That'll be my contribution."

An agreement was reached for a 33-foot cutter, a hard-chine design that would be easy to build. Mary Crowley in California and Jeannot Rey in Tahiti started a fund-raising campaign. I set up a subscription in France with the French Sailing Federation in charge of collecting the funds. One of the most generous donors was Gaston Deferre, the mayor of Marseille.

Three months after the shipwreck, Moitessier had a new 33-foot boat. Wichard, the hardware company, gave him shackles and turnbuckles. Donations came in abundance, providing a pole for the mast and a new mainsail. A shipwright shaped the mast as a gift. A man named Cliff who wanted to build a boat drove all the way from Seattle to visit Moitessier. He wanted to sail with him and in exchange offered him a 12-horsepower diesel engine. Another friend, Jacques Toujan, helped fit out the interior, which was to be very spare and open from stem to stern for space, light, and ventilation. The galley was equipped with the kerosene stove that already had a long history with JOSHUA. Stanchions, pulpits, and the self-steering were installed. The deck arrangement was simple with Attila, the faithful block and tackle, taking the place of winches. All that remained was to name the boat. Bernard suggested Iléana. She wouldn't hear of it and proposed *Tamata*, with a Chinese ideogram painted on the red hull.

At the end of July, seven months after the shipwreck, the unsinkable Moitessier was ready to put back to sea.

20

"Taking part in the creation of the world"

At first Moitessier had thought of going to Mexico or Costa Rica on TAMATA, taking along "typewriter and paper." But in the end, he decided to return to Polynesia. He told me, "In Tahiti, maybe sometimes Moorea, I'll lock myself on board and work seriously." He was hoping to find the same circumstances he had enjoyed when working on *The Long Way.* Would he be able to bring off this book which obsessed him, that he had been talking about for years, and had not even started? The message he wanted to convey was not an easy one.

For 10 months, sailing the most hostile oceans of the world, he'd had an intimate relationship with the sea, the sky, the birds, fishes, and dolphins. As hermits do, when they go to the desert to meditate, Moitessier had made a connection with the Creation. Familiar with the age-old wisdom of Asia, he was able to see the errors the West was making: the frenetic race for money, the materialism, and the negation of spiritual values. Aboard JOSHUA, despite the dangers, the bad weather, and the storms, he felt contented and at peace with the universe, a participant in its immensity. *"I'm really fed up with the false gods of the West. I charge the modern world—that's the monster. It's destroying our earth and trampling the soul of men."*[1]

At the end of his voyage, having completed after two years of work the story of an odyssey that brought him much further than victory, he dreamed of another world run by a hippie president and barefoot ministers guided by their hearts and their instincts. In the hope of contributing to a renewal of conscience, he had attempted to give his royalties to the Pope "to help rebuild the world." He failed utterly. But he didn't get discouraged. He continued unceasingly to fight his battles.

He read; he researched. He asserted, "It's the duty of all of us to participate in the creation of the world." While in Ahé, he was pleased that the French president while wishing a happy New Year to his fellow citizens expressed the hope that they would become more intelligent. For several weeks, he struggled to perfect a three-page letter to Valéry Giscard d'Estaing, the president. While apologizing for his naïveté, he wrote,

May 23, 1979

There are only two roads in life: The high road, the one with a heart where motivations are bigger than man and the low road, the one which, despite all attempts to make it appear otherwise, has no heart, where personal interests dominate.

Worried about the possibilities of war, he expressed another fear:

> Besides the risk of war between the great powers, there is another danger that governments cannot prevent. A well-organized small group who do not believe in anything (and would have expertise in bacteriology for example) would be able to commit unspeakable horrors. Against these acts, no countermeasure is possible, except one: stop the violence at the origin by giving man a true reason to again have faith in humanity.

> I believe that the intelligence of the heart is simply the small creative spirit which adopts the high path . . . Either France will get on a higher plane through the quality of the French people's motives and she will share in the taking off of Europe. Or France will remain what she is and Europe will not take off.

Sending me a copy of this letter, he added in the margin, "I still had a smidgeon of hope." Already in 1977, he had written to a high-ranking government official he knew.

> It has taken me many years to understand that "original sin" and "human stupidity" are synonymous, but with a difference. The idea of original sin implies an absence of responsibility and fatalism. While with human stupidity, this notion of fatalism and absence of

responsibility loses its character since we all know that we are capable of leading ourselves at least in the direction of the beginning of healing, of positive progress, and of fulfillment.

In the letter he sent on June 26, 1984 to Jean Knocker, Bernard, who loved images, illustrated the evolution from primates to man by the *Step of Thought*. He described a bunch of monkeys trying to push a gigantic tree trunk despite the rocks blocking the way and ignoring the few trying to attract their attention. "What those few monkeys, isolated among the crowd, are trying to say is 'let's try something different', for example, let's roll the trunk . . . and this is how the wheel was invented."

In several letters he harked back to the idea that man is constantly presented with a choice. Tom Neale in Suvorov, his own attempt at utopia in Ahé, the invitation to the mayors of villages to plant fruit trees, all show the same concept that won him his nickname "Tamata," try it. *We can create what we want, we can turn nothingness into something that is not nothingness anymore. We always find ourselves between two paths: one plunging into nothingness, the other going toward creation."*[2]

Moitessier's stay in Phil's commune in Israel taught him the precept that, in the manner of Gurdjieff, was founded in meditation and collective work: For creation to happen, a conscious thought must be tied to a conscious act.

Bernard was advocating what, following Samuel Pisar's formula, he called the *Step of Intelligence*. The big problem mankind faced if it did not want to go backward was the "gigantic conflict of Intelligence versus Stupidity."

Impressed by Franz Ait's book, *The Beatitudes, The Total Weapon,* he ordered numerous copies. Using an allegory, as he usually liked to do, he wrote, "The rhesus monkeys have invented matches, and they think they are gods while they are on the brink of setting fire to the whole savanna to solve their internal and neighborhood problems by eliminating in one fell swoop all the rhesus monkeys of the world."

Bernard was also very enthusiastic about Roger Garaudy's book, *L'Appel aux Vivants,* which he considered *"the most important book for our time of change."* He wrote the author on March 18, 1980, telling him how much he admired him, that he hoped the book would be published in paperback for a broader circulation, and concluded with, "Your book contains the Truth in all its simplicity and boundlessness and it is for this reason that it can turn people and move History in the direction of creation. I thank you for having shown me that this is possible through a cry in writing."

It was this "cry" that he wished to express in the book he wanted to write and which he talked about incessantly while never getting started.

In his thoughts about the evolution of the universe, Moitessier was incredibly prescient. At the time of the second oil shock, well before the Gulf War, the attack of September 11, and the war in Iraq, he sent me the following intuitive letter.

July 14, 1979

If one day a country in the West starts an armed operation in Arab territory, this could in turn result in acts of
terrorism coming from small semi-autonomous and fa-
naticized groups . . . I don't know what the West will try
to do, considering the oil. I can only hope that no government head will be stupid enough, while trying to
wrest oil by force (and stupidity), to risk provoking
sooner or later a super terrorist retaliation.

He returned to this problem in a letter he sent on January
6, 1991 to President Mitterand.

The only weapon left for a humiliated or cornered desper-
ado is terrorism. And it is evident that terrorism will (one
day or another) use an atom bomb. This is (or will soon be)
technically feasible. An A-bomb placed for example in a
maid's room in a Western capital and detonated by remote
or other means. Unstoppable. It is unstoppable unless Western moral values finally decide to take charge of today's im-
moral policies of the West. I hope that 1991 will see these
values emerge in our limited conscience.

One of Bernard's obsessions was the nuclear weapons race
between the United States and the USSR. He had lived
through the war in Indochina. He had heard the sound of ma-
chine guns and felt the wind of bullets and he had seen his
former playmates, schoolmates, and best friends of the village

in the Gulf of Siam at the business end of his rifle. Conflicts between nations were unacceptable to him. *"War is the worst monster mankind has ever created. All wars are fratricidal."*[3]

He felt personally affected at the time of the French nuclear testing in Mururoa. A New Zealand yacht, FRI, cruised in the atoll's waters until it was eventually boarded by the French Navy. Iléana had wanted JOSHUA to sail into the area. Bernard had refused because he was afraid he would be evicted from French Polynesia, but he was very impressed to learn that on board FRI was a French general, Brice Lalonde, an ecologist, and that Jean-Jacques Servan-Schreiber (a well-known journalist) had written a series of essays criticizing the tests. While in New Zealand, Bernard had hung out with the crew of the FRI.

During his stay in the United States, the sailor-philosopher, along with other protesters, had worked tremendously hard to further unilateral nuclear disarmament. His friend Ugo noted, "For the first time in the history of mankind, it's possible to be less strong than the adversary and yet be secure."

Bernard stated his position with three points

1. The fear of creating an emotional situation in which a superpower would declare a nuclear war that would get out of control. If the United States decided unilaterally to stop the development of its nuclear weapons, the mutual fear would disappear and with it the risk that the USSR would launch an attack provoked by an emotional factor.

2. By having to maintain only a deterrent force, the United States would free budgetary resources which in turn would allow for the development of the U.S. economy

and consequently the rest of the world, thus reducing social problems.

3. Such an act of courage and intelligence would help the world understand that something new, simple and great was happening.

Moitessier devoted a lot of energy to spreading his ideas. He had leaflets printed and sent over 600 letters to newspapers, magazines, heads of state like Reagan, political figures like Ted Kennedy, and many others. He was pleased to hear Margaret Thatcher declare on the radio that she wished to lessen the tensions with the USSR and limit the United Kingdom's armament to a reasonable level. He congratulated her. In a letter to the Pope in 1984, he conveyed his major worry, "My feeling is that mankind is engaged in the most serious turning point of its history."

In 1987 he rejoiced in the perestroïka started in the USSR by Gorbachev who "is sending us all a huge call to Peace and Reason." He was indignant when Alexandre de Marenches, the former head of the French Secret Service, published an article titled "Gorbachev and the ostriches." He was furious, and wrote to me on January 13, 1990.

People absolutely refuse to open their eyes and look at blinding realities. They see calculations and plots where there is only a desire for peace. It is so much easier and comfortable to hang on to some ancient, completely outdated rules and play the oracle when you are a moron unable to admit that the world is changing. Marenches only

sees a gigantic chess game played by Gorbachev to weaken
Europe, but he is incapable of seeing the formidable hole
that Gorbachev is opening in the concrete wall of human
stupidity.

Moitessier had another hobby. He never forgot what Assam
had taught him in the village in the Gulf of Siam: Chinese
ideograms are the only universal live language in a written
form. Using a small, easy manual, Stephan had started to fa-
miliarize himself with Chinese characters. Bernard wrote the
President of the People's Republic of China.

November 16, 1979

If in the West children were able to learn about two hundred Chinese characters in the ten years of their compul-
sory school attendance, the relationship between East and
West would improve. A spiritual bridge between two
worlds would be created, without harming the culture of
either. I suggest that a group of intellectually honest and
highly competent Chinese try to compose a manual for
teaching these characters in a way both simple and efficient that would appeal to a Western government for
adoption in the classroom.

Nuclear disarmament, fruit trees, Chinese characters, attempt to improve the food crops in Ahé, visits to Suvorov;

these were all part and parcel of the same drive to open people's minds so they could become more intelligent. In admitting that his efforts didn't get the response he was hoping for, Bernard Moitessier was lucid enough to recognize his naïveté. But he was true to his principles—he tried.

1. *The Long Way.*
2, 3. *Tamata and the Alliance.*

21

Return to Tahiti

At the end of July 1983, Moitessier left San Francisco, taking two crew. TAMATA's sea trials went well, and five days of 150 miles or better on the passage to Hawaii proved that the cutter was fast off the wind. Bernard anchored in the lagoon at Keehi. On September 16 he told me he was happy to be back in the tropics.

"I feel much better in Hawaii than in California. Here I can take off when I tire of the place: Polynesia, the Marshall Islands, Mexico, Suvorov."

He met John Hutton again who had opened a shipyard in the islands where he was building steel sailboats. The water was warm, so Bernard swam, and restored his spirits after the nervous exhaustion of the United States and the shipwreck.

Would he be able to write there? He admitted that he felt less and less motivated to write a book as such, but on the other hand, he wrote a large number of letters, and articles that *Cruising World* magazine had commissioned from him. He hoped to find enough money for Iléana and Stephan to spend Christmas with him.

He stayed almost eight months in Hawaii without putting on paper a single line of his book. In May he got ready to sail with two other French boats for the atolls of Palmyra, Penhirn, and Suvorov on a three-month cruise that would bring him to Tahiti. "I am leaving with a very congenial female crew, somewhat hippie, 20 years old, French (unfortunately not much of a cook). She wants to go to Tahiti and also sail (for the first time)," he told me.

While TAMATA had enjoyed 169- and 171-mile days when running, the return to Tahiti was harder, sailing into a stiff trade wind that sometimes reached gale force. The boat pointed to windward quite well despite her shoal draft but she was under-ballasted and tender. In August 1984, TAMATA lay in the berth JOSHUA had left four years earlier at the quay in Papeete, "between the junk and the 'monkey wrench'."

Bernard's first concern was to wash down the interior of the boat and apply three coats of paint so she wouldn't require maintenance for a long time and he could concentrate on his writing. But the work proceeded at a Tahitian pace and by October he still hadn't finished. He had his excuses. "I'm beginning to get back to normal after the four years of nervous tension in the United States. Here, I can finally get back to exercising and swimming every day. I am reviving mentally and physically. All things being equal," he told me, "I'll start with a technical book, that will be very simple and deal strictly with the essential. I think that would be a good preparation for the more serious book that will follow."

At the end of the year, I was supposed to go to Tahiti to interview Moitessier for a program called *Thalassa*. He had agreed and was ready for us to go to sea to take some shots. He ended his January 21, 1985, letter with "It'll be great to see you again." In fact, though we wrote to each other regularly we'd not met since he was in France 10 years earlier, on his way to Israel. On that same trip, in the family home in Les Lecques, he saw his mother for the last time. Marthe Moitessier passed away in November 1983.

During this whole period, Bernard and I played hide and seek across the oceans. When we visited Polynesia in our boat between 1981 and 1983, Bernard lived in California. By the time he arrived in Tahiti in 1984, we'd left for New Caledonia.

In the end, Bernard's interview for *Thalassa* didn't take place. Bernard had formulated the ideas he wanted to expound, and made such demands on the production crew that the project was abandoned. The same happened with an article for *Le Figaro* magazine.

Prior to my coming to Papeete, Bernard wrote to the senior editor of the magazine, reviewing the themes he wanted to discuss—the planting of fruit trees, unilateral nuclear disarmament—and demanding assurance that my interview with him would be on his terms. It became clear that the magazine couldn't comply with his conditions.

Moitessier had very much enjoyed the books written by

Louis Pauwels, *Monsieur Gurdjieff* and *The Morning of the Magicians*. However, since the publication of these works, Pauwels had changed a lot, and Moitessier was very disappointed in his "Open letter to happy people who are right to feel that way."

Would Bernard ever get started on his manuscript? He told me about his procrastinations and the delays they caused.

March 19, 1985

I feel somewhat unbalanced between two poles: on the one hand, a real book (Tamata or the Utopia of Ahé) which scares me because of the enormity of the task, and on the other hand a technical book, which bugs me because of its relative uselessness.

In a letter to his friends on KIM, dated March 18, he admitted, "I miss Iléana and Stephan and their absence is getting me down. I compensate by playing a lot of sports."

Answering his letter, I told him that the technical book was just an excuse. He agreed.

June 14, 1985

I abandoned the technical book after finishing the first chapter. You're probably right. Even if the water is cold, one has to try. I started writing the other book. It's very, very difficult. I wrote barely five pages in two weeks, and I might tear them up.

Finally, the book was under way.

July 11, 1985

I worked every day seriously for a whole month and managed to write the eleven pages of the first chapter. For a week now I've been getting nowhere. I'm trying to do something that's "political" in the greater sense, a Weltanschauung, and this in a language full of poetry and imagery.

In July his friend Ugo, whom he regarded as one of his gurus, came to spend a month on TAMATA. "Here's a guy who had an enormous influence on my vision of the world, a Nobel-prize kind of guy, a scientist, an artist, a poet, and a musician rolled into one. Thanks to him I understood things I couldn't have figured out on my own." They sailed very little, content to go to Moorea, to swim, dive, and above all, to talk.

In September Moitessier left for Suvorov but "not alone . . . She's intelligent, good company, and a good sailor." She was Véronique, an information technician who, after crossing the Atlantic, had been entrusted with delivering a 50-foot schooner to Tahiti. The jaunt to Suvorov ended in frustration. Yachts were no longer allowed there; the Cook Islands had turned it into a surveillance post. TAMATA was only allowed to stay one week. To make up for it, the cruise continued to Bora Bora, Tahaa, and Raiatea.

But he wasn't writing. In his November 26, 1985 letter, Bernard told me of his latest idea.

> I didn't get anywhere with my book, wrote nothing during this escapade. I'm seriously thinking of immersing myself in the ambiance of Paris for a few months, get my book back on track, write in the bistros like I did in the days of *Sailing to the Reefs*. I need a change of air in an atmosphere that will revive me mentally, to feel the cold again for a while after eleven years of not returning to France.

I was skeptical. Over the last ten years, Moitessier had announced many times that he was going to write the book, that he had found the right conditions in which to work on it. This was his latest whim. But why would he have more success in Paris than in Ahé, Moorea, California, Mexico, Hawaii, or Papeete, where each time he said he could do it? And why, when he had written three magnificent books, was he having trouble with this one?

Probably because in his autobiography he would have to describe his Indochina years—his happy childhood in the village, the warmth of life with his Vietnamese and Cambodian friends, and his friendship with the sons of fishermen. Then the tragedy—the massacres, bloodbaths, assassinations, and burning huts of the fratricidal war. He'd have to relive the fear and the hatred, and the suicide of Françou, the brother he loved so much. The hurt was too deep and never healed. Sometimes, he found peace in the solitude of the oceans, where he felt in harmony with the universe. But the wounds had never truly closed.

His memories haunted him; he was full of remorse. Setting forth his experiences in Indochina, as painful as the retelling was, would be a sort of exorcism, a way of laying to rest the horrors he been party to, of getting back in harmony with the world. All the paths he'd taken since turning his back on victory and following *the long way* led toward this reconciliation. The attempt to teach the Paumotus how to improve their way of life, the campaign to plant fruit trees, promoting nuclear disarmament in order to avoid a third world war, all these calls to intelligence and awareness were for him an attempt at therapy.

Writing this book might heal him, if he managed to pull it off.

22

The Alliance

In January 1986, TAMATA lay moored in the Iti Marina at Raiatea, where friends would keep an eye on her. After spending a few days in California with Iléana and Stephan, Bernard landed in Paris seriously determined to concentrate on his book. He wrote to us, "Call me when you are back." In fact, we weren't there to check on the progress of his book. We'd just rounded the Cape of Good Hope and wouldn't be back in Saint Malo, Brittany, where we would complete our circumnavigation, until April.

As soon as he arrived in France, Bernard moved to Véronique's apartment, a studio on rue Ernest Renan, the busiest street in Issy-les-Moulineaux. Would he find in this Paris suburb the inspiration that had eluded him in the tropical sun, the calm of Moorea, and the hectic United States? Most likely the fruits had ripened even if harvesting them would be a long and trying effort. The austere surroundings helped his concentration and at the same time, Bernard found the tool that would make his task easier: the word processor. He first bought an Amstrad, which he later replaced with a portable computer. He backed up his good intentions by reporting his progress in a red notebook.

He never gave up, though, the exercise regimen he needed to maintain his equilibrium. He went swimming regularly, and sweated in the sauna. Often, Dominique Charnay went with him. The young journalist he'd met in Tahiti and taken with him to Ahé proved a faithful friend to the older man. Together they went to the Musée de l'Homme looking for documents on Indochina, and traveled to Deauville to look at the sea and boats.

Suffering but determined, Bernard made progress. He needed help, support, reassurance, and editing as necessary. He sent his manuscript, chapter by chapter, to Dominique Charnay, the sailor Nicole Van de Kerchove, Eric Vibart, a nautical journalist and author who'd written a biography of Gerbault that Moitessier liked, several others, and of course, me, since we'd always exchanged our manuscripts while working on them.

July 30, 1986

Here enclosed are my first two chapters. Chapter 2 gave me a hard time. Three months for fifteen pages!

Side trips brought him some rest. In November 1986, we invited Bernard and Véronique to Saint-Malo so the solo sailor of the Golden Globe could marvel at the high-tech machines in the Route du Rhum and watch the start. In May 1987, they took a short trip to Italy. They visited Jacques-Yves Le Toumelin in his stone house in Le Croisic. Jacques-Yves showed Charnay, who'd come with them, the passage in his book KURUN *autour du monde (*KURUN *Around the World)*, where he mentioned meeting Dominique's father who at the time was the administrator of the Society Islands.

Moitessier sometimes interrupted the writing of *Tamata and the Alliance*, the title he'd already adopted, to send a letter to Mitterrand, Reagan, Cory Aquino, or Yvette Roudy, the Secretary of Women's Rights. "It's high time for women to take charge. They will never do as many stupid things as men." He told us his idea *du jour*, "One of the problems for men is that they are too busy to have the time to think."

In 1987, Bernard and Véronique, who'd been able to take a month's vacation, went back to Polynesia. Bernard arrived a month before Véronique to career and fit out TAMATA. They planned an unusual cruise to Caroline Island, an uninhabited atoll 400 miles north of Tahiti. A couple had decided to move there with their two very young children. Ron, a Scot, had met Anne when she was teaching math in France. Ron was obsessed with settling on a deserted island. The couple had lived on Suvorov, before they were chased away, then in Ahé.

They'd learned about Caroline Island and its unapproachable lagoon from a sailor who'd been shipwrecked there. The only anchorage was at the end of a 30-foot-wide channel that led through the reef to a minuscule dead-end basin. Bernard and Véronique maneuvered TAMATA through the terrifying Blind Passage and anchored her with four anchors. Ron and Anne on FLEUR D'ECOSSE soon followed, loaded with all manner of materials. They helped the "Robinsons" get established, digging a well, building a chicken coop, and clearing the brush where the faré would be built.

This too fast a trip, coming right after the tiring effort of preparing the boat, awoke Bernard's ulcer, entailing a short spell in the hospital in Raiatea.

In May 1988, Moitessier allowed himself a few days' vacation and left for Les Lecques where his youngest brother Gilbert was now living in the family home. He was touched to find a booklet titled *La Digitale*, with only a first name, François. It contained poems written by his brother Françou, published long after his death. He brought back from Les Lecques maps of the village of the Gulf of Siam that Françou had drawn with perfect accuracy and a wealth of detail.

By June 29, Bernard had completed the first 12 chapters of *Tamata and the Alliance*. He was finished with the part on Indochina and the tragic memories. Writing the rest would be easier.

But a storm was about to break over him. Urinary problems prompted him to consult a doctor; tests revealed cancer of the prostate. In Polynesia he had once been diagnosed with cancerous melanoma, caused by his constant exposure to the sun. And now he was under attack from what he would call "The Beast." A new struggle began.

Though he continued to exercise and to swim in Issy-les-Moulineaux's pool, the Beast wouldn't let go. In 1989, he refused to have surgery and accepted his fate. All he wanted was for the disease to allow him time to finish his book. At the end of the year, Véronique bought a fisherman's cottage with a small garden in Kernabat, near Bono, in Brittany. Bernard and Véronique set up house, building their own furniture. Bernard rediscovered his love for the earth and started planting. At the same time, both in Kernabat and in Issy he continued, slowly and laboriously, to write.

February 5, 1990

I'm sending you Chapters 15 and 16. I'd like to get your opinion on these key chapters. I worked a lot (nine months) on both.

In March 1990 his brother Jacky died from liver cancer that had developed with lightning speed. Bernard barely had time to rush to his bedside on the eve of his death.

The return of JOSHUA assuaged his sadness. Reto Fili, to whom Moitessier had given her, had rebuilt her beautifully and took her to Seattle where an American, Johanna Slee, bought her. She was a professional mariner and worked on salmon-fishing boats in Alaska. She sailed JOSHUA solo, and although she'd read *The Long Way* (a copy of the English translation had been on board), she didn't know that her boat was the hero of the Golden Globe. In 1989, she injured her back on a fishing vessel and sold the ketch. A Frenchwoman, Virginia Connor, who was passing through Seattle, thought she recognized JOSHUA and sent a picture to Emmanuel de Toma, a journalist at *Voiles et Voiliers*. Jo Fricaud saw the picture and confirmed it was JOSHUA. Emmanuel de Toma went to Seattle and sailed her in the middle of December with Johanna Slee. Patrick Schnepp, the director of the Maritime Museum of La Rochelle, negotiated JOSHUA's purchase and her return to France by freighter.

In September 1990 Patrick Schnepp and Emmanuel de Toma organized JOSHUA's reception in La Rochelle Harbor. The mythical ketch entered the harbor at the height of the boat show, Moitessier at the helm, and was greeted by an almost religious silence. Bernard, visibly moved, was welcomed by the mayor, Michel Crépeau. Johanna Slee, who had come from Seattle for the occasion, was in tears. To Bernard's great joy, he spent the night alone on JOSHUA. In July 1991, Moitessier, Véronique, Patrick Schnepp, and a crew of friends, brought JOSHUA to Concarneau where in spite of his extreme fatigue, Bernard signed his books at the Maritime Book Fair. One evening, we were all so comfortable in JOSHUA's cabin that nobody wanted to leave and we had to improvise a spaghetti dinner.

1991 was a very difficult year. A blockage of the urinary tract required a small operation. Bernard had lost 13 pounds, his muscles were wasting, and the doctors forbade him to go swimming because the risk of catching an infection at the pool was too great. He underwent urography, scintigraphy, and chemotherapy. His physical exhaustion slowed down the writing. He was fighting not only his sickness but also the ghosts of the past. In August, he tried writing in Brittany, on the beautiful desk he built himself.

August 16, 1991

Here are Chapters 19 and 20. More than a year of work. I'm staying until the end of the month in Kernabat to work on Chapter 21, in the countryside, far away from the noise of traffic. I replaced the pool with gardening and bicycling. I'm beginning to reemerge after my big effort for Chapter 19 and particularly Chapter 20, which was a killer.

But the stay in Brittany didn't help.

August 28, 1991

I completely dried up since the end of Chapter 20. Chapter 21 is still a totally blank piece of paper. On the other hand, the tomatoes are ripening, the zucchini are superb, and the compost heap that I created with love and filled with cow dung + urine and human manure became so hot that the thermometer exploded at 140°F. Writing in the countryside is out as far as I'm concerned. It's time for me to get back to Issy-les-Moulineaux where I'll be stuck between four walls.

Soon Bernard was able to write in more pleasant surroundings. He and Véronique moved to a new apartment in

Vanves, not far from the old one. The fourth-floor, three-room suite on a wide, quiet street, looked out over a large municipal park. In the large living room, canaries from Mozambique flitted from ficus to ficus. The atmosphere was cozy, and Bernard seemed to be in remission.

⚬⚬⚬

In November 1992 Loïck Peyron was preparing for the start of the Vendée Globe, a modern version of the Golden Globe. The boats, the sailors, the atmosphere, and the rules had little in common with the race organized 25 years before by the *Sunday Times*. I arranged a special encounter for *Neptune-yachting*. Bernard went for a sail aboard FUJICOLOR III. The philosopher of the oceans, 67 years old, who'd fled from the media and for whom winning a race meant nothing, met with a very young sprite who oozed confidence in front of a microphone, who'd amassed an impressive number of victories, and who'd just won the singlehanded transatlantic race.

Moitessier had left for a round-the-world race on a sturdy steel ketch with telephone poles as masts, with a sextant to find his position, and armed with a slingshot as his only means of communication. He was now aboard a 60-foot cutter with a carbon hull and spars, fitted with a battery of powerful winches to handle the lines, and bristling with electronic equipment. He took an interest in everything, asking questions, and worrying about the lightness and apparent fragility of a block. He walked barefoot on the deck to get a better feel for the movement of the boat. He was absolutely amazed by the abundance of electronics and communication systems.

He took the helm next to Loïck. The young crew looked on respectfully with touching deference. Moitessier was for them a living legend but he would never put on airs. When getting under way, he started coiling the lines and asked Loïck if he was doing it the right way. Finding the end of a rope was unraveling, he took some thread, got out his knife, and made a tight whipping on it. Nobody had thought of bringing food on this outing in Quiberon Bay, but Bernard took a package of butter cookies out of his pocket and passed it around—he had never forgotten that you did not set sail without something to eat!

After eight and a half years of exhausting work, *Tamata and the Alliance* was almost finished. For what might be the last time, he wanted to go back to his beloved Polynesia. At the end of January 1993, he left with Véronique to join TAMATA. She'd been abandoned for three years, and with Veronique dedicating herself to the boat's care, they refitted her. Bernard wrote to me

April 25, 1993

We rented a faré less than a mile from the marina. We each have a bicycle. I started writing the last chapter two weeks ago. I work at it every day. It's well on its way.

We've rented the place until the end of June, view over the sea, our feet in the water. It really is a beautiful place. Perfect happiness for the last run.

The last chapter was finally done. A small crew from *Thalassa*, including Jean Loiseau and Denis Bassompierre, the cameraman, came to do a show on Moitessier. For a week they filmed TAMATA tacking up and down Tahaa's lagoon, and Bernard climbing a coconut tree, showing that, despite his sickness, he was fit and strong. Polynesia continued to fascinate him.

August 12, 1993

Véronique and I have been dreaming more and more of returning to Polynesia for quite a while. She is enthralled with photography and video and would like to try her luck professionally in the field. I could start working at the same time on a technical book Sea-Boats-the Life of a Robinson on an Atoll. The Beast has granted me a truce since I came back.

Because of the after effects of chemotherapy, he had to completely shield his skin from the sun by wearing pants, a long-sleeved shirt, and a hat. During one of his previous stays, he'd made his peace with Deshumeurs. After *the long way*, his accomplice on SNARK, who now lived in Tahiti, had cast doubts on what Bernard had claimed he'd done, creating a deep rift between them.

The Alliance

---oeo---

Bernard returned to Paris at the end of October for the publication of *Tamata and the Alliance*. The book was immediately a huge success. He gave many interviews. Philippe Gildas, the journalist who, he'd said, "had fire in his belly," invited him to the show *Nulle part ailleurs* (Nowhere else). Bernard had sent each chapter as he was writing them to Roger Garaudy who quoted in his book *Mon tour du monde en solitaire (My Solo Circumnavigation)* the letter Bernard had sent him from Polynesia. During a show, Garaudy said of Bernard, "Bernard is a man who feels solidarity with Everything. When he talks about gods and dragons, I feel that we have the same gods, the same dragons. He taught me to regard the sea as a parable, a metaphor for God's presence, the Infinite."

At the Boat Show, where Bernard was signing copies of his book, the bookseller quickly ran out of them. A visitor introduced herself to him, "I am Marie-Thérèse." Bernard recognized in this good-looking woman in her sixties, with her curly blond hair, the love of his youth, his fiancée from Indochina after whom he'd named his boats.

Knowing he was nearing his end and accepting it calmly, Moitessier reconnected with the happiness of earlier times. *Voiles et Voiliers* offered to take him to Vietnam, to the places of his childhood. He was hesitant. "I would love to go if there is free travel in this dictatorship." To reassure him, we invited him for lunch with Jean-Claude Guillebaud who had just been to Vietnam with the photographer Raymond Depardon.

In February 1994, accompanied by Daniel Allisy, editor of

the magazine and Eric Vibart, Bernard rediscovered the markets of Saigon and the aromas of his youth. He squatted to eat soup, and followed the road the family car, the Hotchkiss, had taken to the village where he'd spent such happy days. He stayed there only one day. In the magazine's article about this pilgrimage into his past, Vibart wrote, "To return to the village is going back to sit next to Xaï, the friend for ever, the Vietnamese brother." Retracing the footsteps of his childhood, Bernard climbed the stairs of his parents' house, visited the huts again, and stretched out on a platform to exchange memories in Vietnamese with the old timers who'd never forgotten him. "Bernard can now walk in peace on the village path. Through different roads, in a roundabout way, Bernard and the village are now joined by the Alliance."

The trip wasn't entirely pleasant. Bernard caught cholera and had to be hospitalized for a few days in Saigon. After he returned from Vietnam, the Beast redoubled its assaults. Bernard still hoped to write the technical book he'd been thinking about for so long, but it wasn't published until after his death, thanks to Véronique's work in organizing his articles, notes, and appendices.

Having no illusions as to the state of his health, he asked Charnay for an estate lawyer and wrote his will. In April he was admitted to the oncology department of Gustave Roussy Hospital.

At the hospital, and then at the Vanves apartment, his family and friends succeeded one another at his bedside: Iléana and Stephan from California, his brother Gilbert, Marie-Thérèse, Jocelyne and René Tournouer, old friends from

Tahiti, and of course Dany and I. Just as Bernard was leaving the hospital, Françoise arrived from Marseille and, with her daughter, came to visit her former husband. "Bernard is lying on a sofa, shivering under a sad blanket of gray cotton, his face drawn, skin and bones, white, white hair," she said. She hadn't seen him in 20 years.

In May, *The Life of Bernard Moitessier According to Astrology*, was published. The author, Marie-Jeanne Kraft, an astrologer, had learned about Moitessier by reading *The Long Way*, met him, and became intrigued by his life. "Who were those people for whom the call of the sea was transformed into an initiation?"

Bernard hardly left the bed on which he lay in an old sweater and with a sarong covering his naked legs. He asked his female visitors to massage his feet and legs because they were always cold.

His contract with Editions Arthaud and the success of *Tamata and the Alliance* that sold a hundred thousand copies within a few months gave him a financial ease he wasn't used to. He was very generous, but not always with good judgment. People I didn't know came to the apartment, passing shadows perhaps attracted by the smell of money, and hippies who kept Bernard in marijuana. A healer came up with a surprising diagnosis, suggested strange treatments, and took off with a check. More appropriately, Bernard helped the oceanographer Anita Conti, who really needed it. Bernard ebbed away, serenely, at peace with himself and with the world. He had vanquished the Dragon, concluded his Alliance with the Universe, and wrote at the end of his book, *"It's never a mistake to forgive."*

I gave him a last kiss on June 15. He was lucid, but very weak. He set sail the next day on his last cruise.

—◦◦◦—

There were many of us in the little harbor of Bono, in the Gulf of Morbihan, who had come to pay tribute to Bernard Moitessier. The women who had loved him were there, Marie-Thérèse, Françoise, Iléana, and Véronique, who'd wanted a Tahitian ceremony. Stephan attended, deeply moved. JOSHUA had been brought from La Rochelle and was moored alongside the quay. We read passages from his books. I tried to say a few words, but my voice was choked with sadness. "When we are at sea, you will always be the wave lulling our hull, the dolphin playing at the prow, the flying fish jumping before the stem, the seagull soaring above the wake."

Family and friends threw flower petals on the sea as a last farewell.

The casket was carried to the small cemetery on top of the hill, close by the sea. Moitessier's long way was at an end.

Drawing Moitessier used in his letters and dedications

The Boats of
Bernard Moitessier

Reprinted from
A Sea Vagabond's World
by Bernard Moitessier

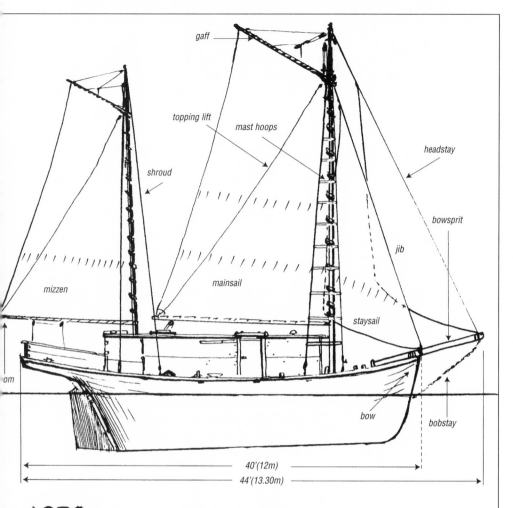

gaff

topping lift

mast hoops

headstay

shroud

bowsprit

jib

mizzen

mainsail

staysail

om

bow

bobstay

40'(12m)

44'(13.30m)

1950
Snark

Wooden gaff-rigged ketch. A Malaysian boat, known as a *proa*—which is very different from a junk—built in Borneo for fishing. She had a bowsprit and not much freeboard. Length 40'; beam 14'; draft 6'.

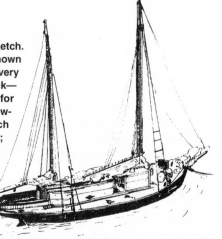

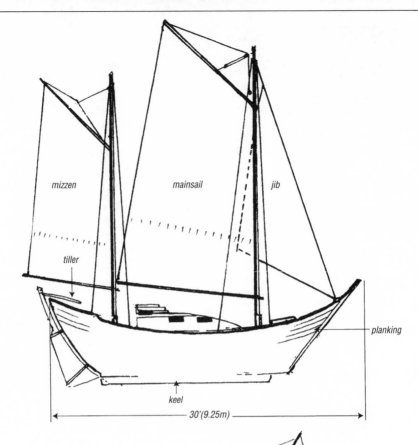

mizzen

mainsail

jib

tiller

planking

keel

30'(9.25m)

She was a beautiful Gulf of Siam junk, sturdy and rounded, smelling sweetly of wood oil. Her sharply angled bow gracefully extended her strong sheer forward, pointing to the sky, the horizon . . . and the lands beyond that horizon.

1952
Marie-Thérèse

A traditional wooden junk, gaff-rigged, with a very tall, slender bow and internal ballast. Length 30'; beam 10'.

1955
Marie-Thérèse II

Of Asian inspiration and built by eye, without any plans, she had rounded lines. *Marie-Thérèse II* was a ketch, initially gaff-rigged, then Marconi. Handsome mahogany keel, bow, and stem pieces; jackfruit and guava wood ribs; laminated deck beams. She had 880 pounds (400 kg) of exterior ballast; the rest was interior and fixed. Length 27'; width 10'; draft 5'.

5'(1.50m)

10'(3.15m)

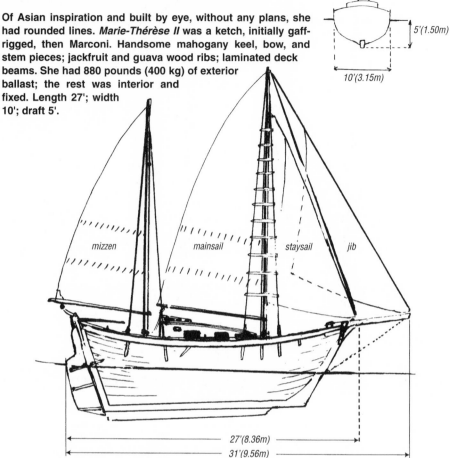

mizzen   mainsail   staysail   jib

27'(8.36m)

31'(9.56m)

Maintaining my wooden boats presented some tricky problems that required solid credentials: you had to be a "doctor of rot," "doctor of shipworms," and "doctor of leaks" . . . Despite my instinctive distrust, I was forced to compare wood and steel. Working on a freighter taking me back from the Caribbean to France in 1958, those three doctorates were replaced by a scraper, a can of paint, and a big brush, with no further qualifications required beyond a little good will . . . I learned that a steel boat's topsides don't rust when they are maintained in the time-honored merchant marine way: painting, painting, and more painting, using quick-drying paint, since you're always in a hurry to get underway.

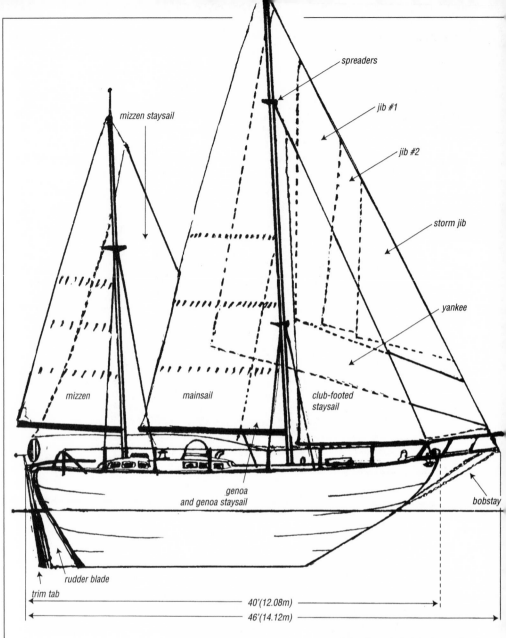

mizzen staysail

spreaders

jib #1

jib #2

storm jib

yankee

mizzen

mainsail

club-footed
staysail

genoa
and genoa staysail

bobstay

rudder blade

trim tab

40'(12.08m)

46'(14.12m)

1961
Joshua

Joshua is a 40-foot steel ketch designed by Jean Knocker and built for me by Jean Fricaud in his yard at Chauffailles. Steel had turned out to be the best answer to my concerns about maintenance and strength. From our very first meeting, Knocker put me at ease. I made plan

and section sketches to scale. He then drew the waterlines, corrected my mistakes to conform to the requirements of naval architecture, and produced a real architect's plan that suited my wishes. This work together stretched over fourteen months, until the plans were done to his and my satisfaction.

Needless to say, Knocker put in a great deal of work, given the number of requirements I had for the boat:

1. Good upwind performance. From the point of view of sailing close-hauled, my previous boats weren't much good. And when the seas were stronger than the wind, performance became pitiful, especially with a bit of contrary current. That state of affairs can lead to catastrophe, because it is very tiring to tack day and night. Fatigue leads to exhaustion, and that can put a boat on the rocks.

2. Shallow draft (things are getting complicated already). This is an element of both safety and pleasure in coral seas, where a boat drawing only 4'6" can get much closer to shore and enter little protected coves whose passes are too shallow for a boat with 6-foot draft. Knocker suggested a very elegant solution involving a centerboard, but I wouldn't hear of a centerboard well, since at the time I intended to use cold-molded wood construction.

3. Norwegian stern. I prefer a pointed Norwegian stern because it can very effectively divide, direct, and ease a breaking sea's violent push when running.

4. Very comfortable interior, but divided between two totally independent cabins (another difficulty, since the Norwegian stern makes the aft cabin less roomy).

5. Marconi ketch rig (this is awkward for the aft cabin, because of the mizzen mast).

6. Stern-hung rudder, which lets you directly connect a self-steering device.

As you see, the architect found himself confronted with an imbroglio of demands, which made his task very difficult. Good windward performance requires a fairly deep draft. Also, the least possible windage, whereas I wanted to be able to stand up anywhere in the main cabin, and in part of the aft cabin. But Knocker was able to overcome these serious difficulties.

Joshua: Length 40' plus a 6-foot bowsprit; length at the waterline 36'; beam 12'; draft 5'. Steel used: frames: 2" x 3/16" flat iron. Keel: 9/32" plate for the sides, 13/16" for the bottom. Stem and sternpost: 3" x 13/16" flat iron. Strakes: 3/16". Garboard: 7/32". Deck frames: 2" x 3/16" flat iron, on edge.

1982

If JOSHUA *were 32 feet long and well laid out, she would be plenty of boat for two people, plenty to set out to sea on, and would require less time and money to maintain and outfit . . .*

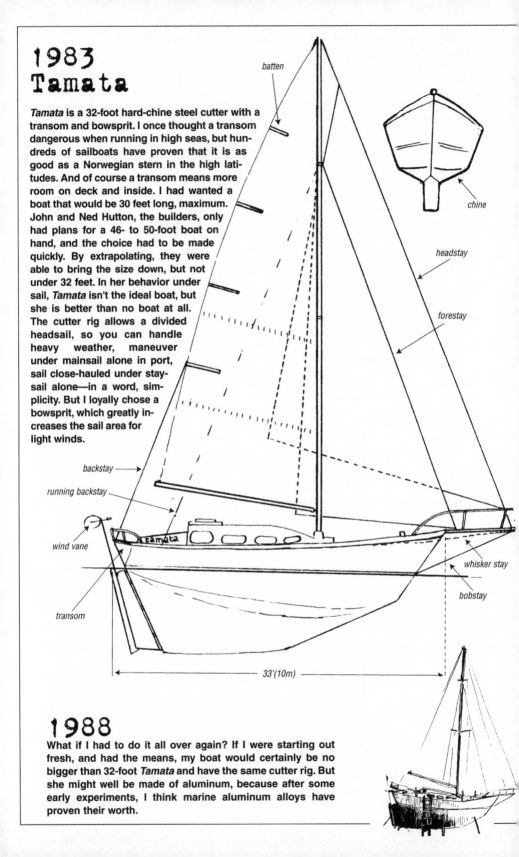

1983
Tamata

Tamata is a 32-foot hard-chine steel cutter with a transom and bowsprit. I once thought a transom dangerous when running in high seas, but hundreds of sailboats have proven that it is as good as a Norwegian stern in the high latitudes. And of course a transom means more room on deck and inside. I had wanted a boat that would be 30 feet long, maximum. John and Ned Hutton, the builders, only had plans for a 46- to 50-foot boat on hand, and the choice had to be made quickly. By extrapolating, they were able to bring the size down, but not under 32 feet. In her behavior under sail, *Tamata* isn't the ideal boat, but she is better than no boat at all. The cutter rig allows a divided headsail, so you can handle heavy weather, maneuver under mainsail alone in port, sail close-hauled under staysail alone—in a word, simplicity. But I loyally chose a bowsprit, which greatly increases the sail area for light winds.

batten

chine

headstay

forestay

backstay

running backstay

wind vane

transom

whisker stay

bobstay

33'(10m)

1988
What if I had to do it all over again? If I were starting out fresh, and had the means, my boat would certainly be no bigger than 32-foot *Tamata* and have the same cutter rig. But she might well be made of aluminum, because after some early experiments, I think marine aluminum alloys have proven their worth.

Chronology

Dates in Bernard Moitessier's life

April 10, 1925   Bernard Moitessier is born in Hanoi, Indochina.
1947   Coastal shipping aboard a junk in the Gulf of Siam.
1951   Cruise from Vietnam to Singapore and back with Pierre Deshumeurs on SNARK.
1952   Solo departure from Cambodia aboard the junk MARIE-THÉRÈSE. Shipwreck on a reef in the Chagos Bank.
1953–1955   Construction in Mauritius of the ketch MARIE-THÉRÈSE II. Departure from Mauritius.
1955–1958   Stopovers in South Africa. Crossing of the Atlantic Ocean. Shipwreck in the Caribbean.
1958   Arrival in Paris.
1959   Publication of *Sailing to the Reefs*. Marriage to Françoise.

1961-1962	Construction of JOSHUA
1963-1966	Cruise Marseille-Tahiti, followed by Tahiti-Alicante non-stop via Cape Horn, with Françoise.
1967	Publication of *Cape Horn: the Logical Route*
1968-1969	Participation in the Golden Globe. Solo non-stop race one and a half times around the world. Arrival in Tahiti.
1970-1971	Meeting with Iléana and birth of Stephan Moitessier. Publication of *The Long Way*
1975	Cruise to Suvorov. Visits to New Zealand and Israel.
1975-1978	He settles on Ahé, an atoll in the Tuamotus, then on Moorea in August 1978.
1980	Campaign for the planting of fruit trees along the roads. Departure for California.
1982	JOSHUA is wrecked by a hurricane in Cabo San Lucas, Mexico.
1983	Construction of TAMATA. Return to Polynesia via Hawaii and Suvorov.
1985	Meeting with Véronique.
1986	Return to France.
1990	JOSHUA becomes part of the Maritime Museum of La Rochelle. Publication of *Tamata and the Alliance*. Voyage to Vietnam.
June 16, 1994	Death of Bernard Moitessier
1995	Publication of *A Sea Vagabond's World*
1998	Publication of the English edition of *A Sea Vagabond's World*

Bibliography

Charnay, Dominique. *Moitessier: le chemin des îles.* Grenoble: Glénat, 1999

Chichester, Sir Francis. GIPSY MOTH IV *circles the world.* New York: Coward Mc Cann, 1968

Knox-Johnston, Robin. *A World of My Own.* New York: W.W. Norton, 1970

Kraft, Marie-Jeanne. *La vie de Bernard Moitessier à travers son thème astral.* St. Malo: L'Ancre de Marine, 1994

Lerebours, Véronique. *Bernard Moitessier au fil des rencontres.* Paris: Arthaud, 2204

Merrien, Jean. *Les Navigateurs solitaires.* Paris: Denoël, 1953

Moitessier, Bernard, translated by Inge Moore. *Cape Horn: The Logical Route.* Dobbs Ferry, NY: Sheridan House, 2003

Moitessier, Bernard, translated by William Rodarmor. *The Long Way.* Dobbs Ferry, NY: Sheridan House, 1995

Moitessier, Bernard, translated by René Hague. *Sailing to the Reefs.* Dobbs Ferry, NY: Sheridan House, 2001

Moitessier, Bernard, translated by William Rodarmor. *A Sea Vagabond's World.* Dobbs Ferry, NY: Sheridan House, 1998

Moitessier, Bernard, translated by William Rodarmor. *Tamata and the Alliance.* Dobbs Ferry, NY: Sheridan House, 1995

Moitessier de Cazalet, Françoise. *60,000 Milles à la voile.* Saint-Malo: L'Ancre de Marine, 1999

Neale, Tom. *An Island to Oneself: Six Years on a Desert Island.* UK: Wm.Collins, 1966

Nichols, Peter. *A Voyage for Madmen.* New York, NY: Harper Collins, 2001

Smeeton, Miles. *Once is Enough.* Dobbs Ferry, NY: Sheridan House, 1991

Tomalin, Nicholas and Ron Hall. *The Strange Last Voyage of Donald Crowhurst.* London, UK: Hodder and Stoughton Ltd. 1970

Neptune nautisme, June 1966

Neptune-yachting, March 1988

Voiles et Voiliers, April 1994